RECLAIMING *the* SEALSKIN

RECLAIMING *the* SEALSKIN

MEDITATIONS IN THE CELTIC SPIRIT

Annie Heppenstall-West

WILD GOOSE PUBLICATIONS

www.ionabooks.com

First published 2002 by
Wild Goose Publications
Fourth Floor, Savoy House, 140 Sauchiehall Street,
Glasgow G2 3DH, UK
Wild Goose Publications is the publishing division of the Iona Community.
Scottish Charity No. SCO03794. Limited Company Reg. No. SCO96243.

ISBN 1 901557 66 9

Cover design © 2002 David Gregson
Seal photo ©1997 DigitalStock
Meditation cards © Annie Heppenstall-West

Wild Goose Publications gratefully acknowledges the support of the Drummond Trust, 3 Pitt Terrace, Stirling FK8 2EY, UK, in producing this book.

Overseas distribution
Australia: Willow Connection Pty Ltd, Unit 4A, 3-9 Kenneth Road, Manly Vale, NSW 2093
New Zealand: Pleroma, Higginson Street, Otane 4170, Central Hawkes Bay
Canada: Novalis Publishing & Distribution ....

Permission to reproduce any part of this work in Australia or New Zealand should be sought from Willow Connection.

Produced by Reliance Production Company, Hong Kong
Printed and bound in China

ACKNOWLEDGEMENTS

Reclaiming the Sealskin was written gradually over almost two decades, a record of my responses to the people, places, events and situations I encountered. Without these multifarious influences, some enjoyable and some disturbing (some both at the same time), there may well have been nothing to write about. So I am grateful to everybody whom I have met along the way, especially to the people who have always supported me, but including the ones who – one way or another – have given me a hard time! In particular I would like to thank my husband Jared, for his honest (and very valuable) opinion and for his help with the computer; my son Luke, for his unique and delightful exploration of childhood; and my parents for their encouragement and for the use of and advice on their extensive library of obscure books, especially concerning references to ancient languages. I would also like to thank my sisters: Jane for reading the first contemplation to be put into print and telling me to carry on; Mary for her shining example of level-headedness; and my dear soul-friend Juliette, with whom I have always felt safe sharing my faith, and Jo, archetypal wild woman. Sandra Kramer, Publishing Manager of Wild Goose Publications, should also receive special mention, for being the first person to read *Reclaiming the Sealskin*, and for being so positive and sensitive in guiding me towards publication.

CONTENTS

PART 1
SEARCHING FOR THE SEALSKIN

INTRODUCTION

'But ask the animals, and they will teach you;
the birds of the air, and they will tell you;
ask the plants of the earth,
and they will teach you;
and the fish of the sea will declare to you.
Who among all of these does not know
that the hand of the Lord had done this?
In his hand is the life
of every living thing
and the breath of every human being.'

Job 12:7–10 (NRSV)

HERE WERE ONCE SELKIES, according to Scottish folklore, who for the most part swam as seals in the ocean. Just like true seals, they were entirely at one with the water, able to remain submerged for considerable lengths of time between breaths, able to hunt and dive down deep into the cool darkness. They had smooth coats and called out in the eerie, wistful call that wild creatures share; for they were wild and belonged at sea. On certain still evenings the selkies would shuffle up onto the shore and there shed their soft sealskins. While true seals are cumbersome on land, a selkie without its skin had the form of a graceful and strong-limbed human. Being wild, they danced as naked and as innocently unashamed as Adam and Eve before they tasted that forbidden fruit. Now, tradition has it that a selkie could be captured and domesticated simply by taking possession of the sealskin. Thus it happened that young selkies, often but not always women, were trapped and tricked into leaving the sea for a life on land. They would live a quiet life, even bearing human children, but at the depths of their soul was a deep hunger, a yearning that no human love could satisfy, a longing to be back in the sea. Compassionate souls might eventually realise the cause of the creature's sadness and restore the sealskin; several stories tell of the children themselves setting their mothers free. But there are more disturbing tales of people who destroyed the sealskin in an attempt to make captivity permanent, but in so doing inadvertently destroyed their stolen selkie too.

The human soul is in some way like a selkie robbed of its skin. She knows that she belongs somewhere else; she knows there is something more, something huge and wonderful, something that can hold her completely, just as she was held so safe in the little ocean of her mother's womb. We know that there is more to life than meets the eye and we can never be truly at peace until we too find our true home. The longing of the selkie is an analogy for the soul's longing to return to the 'ocean' of God.

So where can we search for our sealskins? Of course they are well hidden, because the one that took them meant us to stay on dry land. Should we dig in the ground, or turn our homes upside-down? Maybe! But who is the one who trapped us? How did it happen? Why do we have no memory of it? Perhaps we were babies when we were stolen, or perhaps we are older than we remember. Who are we but selkies with amnesia? Much ink has been spilt on the perpetual search for some clue to our being, some key to freedom. But all the books in the land cannot answer the soul's deepest questions of life's meaning*, for they cannot be articulated in written words, and words alone do not unlock the soul. The soul speaks the same wild language as the creatures and we have simply to live. Or, to rephrase, we have to live simply.

Reclaiming the Sealskin is very much bound up with the soul's search for meaning, the selkie's hunt for her stolen skin. She will search every nook and cranny like the woman of the gospels who lost a coin. In a way, *Sealskin* is a catalogue of discoveries, of the things we might find under the stones as we turn them; the little things we find swept under the carpet and buried in the sand. The process of searching has value in itself; it forces us to clarify what it is we are looking for. The woman who lost a coin found it in her own house. In the folk tales of Scotland, the selkie would often find her skin at home too, tucked under the rafters or buried under the hearth stones. In our own quests, perhaps we too can hope to find that precious kingdom of God much closer than we had dared to hope. Success, after all, depends on being able to recognise the object of our search. Thus, I have tried to express a synthesis with Christian faith of the meaning we find in the life around us, and with an abiding respect for the biblical texts which give us true reason for hope. At times I have begun by looking at a feature of the natural world, or a simple human-made object, turning it over in my hands and my thoughts until some connection with the scriptures occurs to me. At other times I have begun with a biblical quotation, feeling it to be of pivotal importance, and have mulled it over until a symbol presents itself. The quotation from Job, at the beginning of the chapter, invites us to ask the animals, the birds of the air, the plants of the earth, the fish of the sea, which is what I have tried to do. For the creatures and the plants have a voice, if only we can forget human speech and listen, and they will lead us on in our search for the sealskin, for our freedom. The natural world sings with the sheer energy and enthusiasm (in the true sense of the word) of life, and we can use it to teach us.

Selkie,
the ocean of God has never forgotten you
and is calling you back
as the waves lap the shore.
Your soul compels you
to reclaim your sealskin,
to reclaim your freedom,
to dive deep down into the bliss of your home.

*Some would argue that the Bible holds the answers. Well, the anthology of writings that we call the Bible *can* have the answers, but it depends rather how we read it. It can also be used to justify social outrages that we cannot tolerate today such as sexual discrimination, racial favouritism and anti-Semitism. A twisted and disturbed heart will scour the pages for words of wrath and condemnation, the anger of the individual seeking reflection in holy scripture, portraying a God of terror and judgement. A gentle soul will seek words of comfort and love, and a soul caught up in a struggle for justice will find fighting talk of righteousness. When we come to the Bible full of our own opinions, then our own opinions are very often reflected back to us. It can be a shock to find passages that contradict us or even each other, although we should not expect the wide range of texts presented in the Bible to be entirely self-consistent. A religious text must be read with an open mind and an open heart for it to have any real value, and also with some idea of the context in which it was written, for we are not seeking self-justification but the truth.

SETTING OFF, BACK DOWN TO EARTH

He (Jesus) also said to the crowds, 'When you see a cloud rising in the west, you immediately say, "It is going to rain"; and so it happens. And when you see the south wind blowing you say, "There will be scorching heat"; and it happens … You know how to interpret the appearance of the earth and sky, but why do you not know how to interpret the present time?'

Luke 12:54–56 (NIV)

Jesus constantly referred to the natural world in his teachings; he found meaning and symbolism all around him. The gospels abound with sheep, fig trees, mustard seeds, mountains, donkeys and lamplight. He had an affinity with nature that he would have shared with his first-century village companions; the quotation above demonstrates the weather lore that was commonly understood. Elsewhere we read for example how Jesus's knowledge of the Sea of Galilee enabled him to see the tell-tale surface ripples that indicated a shoal of fish were nearby (John 21:6). Other passages reveal his tender reflections on lost lambs and chicks nestled with their mother hen. Nature didn't just provide teaching material, Jesus was obviously moved by the world around him. Why else would he go into the mountains to pray, alone at night with the wild beasts, unless he felt at ease with such an environment, and closer to God? Nature moves us too, but something happened in the history of Christianity that created unease at the thought of loving nature too much. There is a terrible skeleton in the ecclesiastical cupboard of witch-hunts and the burning of wise old women, a terrible fear of magic and an association between many familiar animals and plants and the devil. Even pictures of the devil started to look very like the old nature god Pan. But fear of magic is a demonstration of belief in its power. There is no power in magic; it is simply the physical projection of people's will. It is the misguided attempt to manipulate nature for a person's own ends. Christians know that God alone has true power, and therefore magic and superstition are meaningless. They need hold no fear. As for the wise women, what crime did they commit but to pass on the ancient lore of healing herbs in an attempt to cure pain and heartache? In the witch-hunts much of our folk tradition died and a culture emerged based on fear, mistrust and hysteria. It was dangerous to be seen in the woods gathering herbs, it was dangerous to live alone with an old cat, it was dangerous to be the wart-troubled relative of a farmer whose eggs all addled. It seems ridiculous to us now, but the legacy remains and is insidious.

Christians sometimes – perhaps even subconsciously – feel a little ill at ease in bonding too closely with nature. But they can be reassured, for the Bible itself abounds in natural imagery, likewise the artwork, poetry and prayers attributed to the early Christian communities of the British Isles. Feeling close to and being moved by creation is not the same as worshipping or deifying nature. The current interest in so-called Celtic Christianity, whether at an intellectual level or as an inspiration for devotion, is perhaps connected to some extent with the deep desire to rediscover something older than current denominational divisions, something simpler and intrinsically beautiful. It doesn't mean that we can (or would want to) re-create the past, nor does it mean that we are discrediting what we have at the moment. It means allowing the wisdom there at our roots to nurture our growth in the present and into the future. We are always free to explore our spiritual heritage and to bring it into our own place of worship now, just as we are free to explore the natural world we encounter all around us.

It is one thing to know the history of an ancient movement on an intellectual level, yet another to study and appreciate the cultural delights of that movement – its art, poetry and music for example – and quite something else again to live the life espoused by that movement. You can look from the outside, objectively, perhaps critically, and you can look from the inside. There are many excellent books on the saints, history and arts of the old Celtic Christianity, which of course ought to be read, for we should seek to gain knowledge of that which we want to understand. There are places to go and people to meet who will welcome us and show us their own way of making Celtic Christianity alive in a new and dynamic way, for a modern-minded people. These people and places are there to support our growth and by all means we should glean from the wisdom and richness in Spirit that they cultivate. But, at the end of the day, we each have to find our own unique expression of what life means to us; we have to think for ourselves how the teachings of a Palestinian Jew of the first century relate to us, to our world and to our lives. We have to find a way of living our lives on a normal day-to-day basis that brings us closer to creation and closer to the heart of God. So, for the times when you feel alone; for the times when you feel unsupported and uncertain; for the times when you feel your own journey is leading you along a narrow and long-forgotten path: take heart that God is all around you. The narrow path is the one that leads home. The Celtic saints lived a life very close to the poverty and humble strength of Christ, and if they could feel close to Christ then perhaps we can learn something from their approach to the world.

SOUL JOURNEY: A GUIDED MEDITATION

'...There you saw how the Lord your God carried you, as a father carries his son, all the way you went until you reached this place.'

— Deuteronomy 1:31 (NIV)

The following is a meditation introducing key themes which feature in subsequent pages. It is an opportunity to allow the hungry intellect to be still, and to give imagination free rein. Exercising our imagination is a way to unlock the dynamic, creative aspect of our spirituality, the realm of vision, mystical revelation and insight. A whole world of imagery, allegory and new meaning is available to us once we open the door.

Look around the place where you are at this moment. Notice all the modern things around you. What are they for? How much effort was invested in making them? What happens when you discard them? Do they go back to the earth like bones and bark? Or will they end up in a landfill site? You might pause for a moment to consider your own impact on the earth: the elements of your lifestyle that pollute and exploit; the elements that show respect and appreciation. Focus on the natural processes of death and regeneration, on the vulnerability of life. Focus on the ancient exhortation to tread lightly on the earth. You know we have to restore our relationship with the earth; let your love envelop the world. Look again at your room, your home, all the material things around you. As your eye rests on each object, allow your sense of gratitude to be awakened.

Now, let your mind settle on something from the natural world. There must be something in the room, if only a wooden table. There is a door in your imagination. Go through it, taking with you your natural object. If it is large, take only a token part, such as a leaf. Shut all those worrying things from the modern world behind the door and leave the whole lot, just for now. You are alone with your natural object. What is it? Where does it come from? See it in the beauty of its simple state: a stone, a stick or leaf, a shell, a jar of water, a flower, the wool from a sheep. You are ready to walk, but wait! There is a strange old bundle lying on the ground at your feet. You have a sudden sensation like a child rediscovering an old and much-loved toy, a feeling of gladness, of freedom. These feelings are bound up with the bundle; it is so precious to you. This is the thing you had always had at the back of your mind, a sense that there was something to look for, something you had to remember. Here it is. Take the bundle and your natural object now, and walk. You find you are walking over soft grass, you have bare feet. When did you last walk barefoot on the grass? Maybe you will have a memory from childhood or an association with having fun or relaxing.

Walk on but look out for tree roots as the grass gives way to soil; we are entering the woodland. Sunlight filters through the canopy of green, trunks soar upwards like pillars in a cathedral, their leaves drinking in the light, their roots gripping the earth. Touch a tree. Do you know what it is? Feel the rough bark, the vibrant life flowing underneath. Stop and listen to birdsong, the rustle of squirrels in the leaf litter, insects buzzing; feel a breeze stirring the branches, your hair and clothes. You are at peace here but you know there is something drawing you on. Go on through the woods, delight in the bluebells, let creatures come and go without fear. What do you see? One animal or bird might come up to you. Are you surprised? Are you afraid? Might you or it speak? Does it follow you now, or does it take the lead? Whatever, let it come with you to the edge of the wood, and as you walk think what quality that creature and yourself share that drew you together.

The path continues across a meadow until you find you are on a track heading down to the seashore. Go to the beach; do you find pebbles or sand, high tide or low? Look out to sea. Is it calm, or turbulent? Somewhere nearby, you have some kind of boat moored. Get in the boat. Feel it take your weight and roll a little, but know you are safely supported. You can allow a twinge of anticipation for you sense that you are drawing closer to what you seek. Your boat makes progress over the sea. As you reach the deeper waters you notice seals playing nearby, diving and bobbing up, totally at one with the sea. How would it be to swim with the seals? Now, a faint memory surfaces. You suddenly realise what the bundle is. Untie it; shake out the folds and slip on your supple sealskin. Trapped on the dry land so long, you had almost forgotten your true nature and the depths calling to you. Go now; slip into the water and dive down. There is another world down here, untouched by the superficial life on the surface. This is where you want to be. Enjoy the sensation of fluid movement and all-embracing water. Connect with your womb life – of course there is a connection – to a place that is at once the gateway to your greatest spiritual depth and the point of communion with your own conception, your own beginning. You have come to your beginning place, in two ways. You spiral down, down, always spiralling, seeking something. What is it you want? What does anybody ultimately want but peace, enlightenment, love, endless joy, freedom and true wisdom?

Ahead of you is a cave mouth. Go in. You find that inside there is an air pocket – you may breathe! Take deep breaths like the seal-swimmer you are, just surfaced from a long underwater stretch. The cave is lit somehow from above; there must be an aperture in the rock letting in sunlight. The shaft of light illuminates two figures, a kind and very ancient woman (let it be an old man if you prefer!) and a little child. Surely a person so old and seeming so gentle must have the insight you seek, so ask her: 'Wise one, help me see things the way they really are.' You are surprised and maybe a little affronted when the child and then the sage burst into laughter. 'You want to see things the way they really are?' asks the old woman. 'Well between us we have but three true-seeing eyes! We have the two bright eyes of the child, who describes all the wonder she sees for me to imagine, and my one seeing eye, which looks not outwards but within. The child is my outward eye; I am the child's inner eye. We are the guardians of true insight. We live in your heart; you are our home.'

You sense it is time to go but before you leave remember you still have your natural object with you. It is a child's gift, so give it to the child. She will cherish it just for the moment. Now you can come back, knowing your simple gift is accepted, just as you are. Curiously, you find now that the cave has a tunnel that leads you right back to the door that you closed. Your journey took you through a spiral like a snail shell, where the whole is united by a core, an axis, a central pivot like the supporting column of a spiral staircase. You can travel the long way, but you are always connected to the hub, that cave deep under the sea of your spiritual questing. But what of the sealskin? Well, now you have reclaimed it, you are in control again. You can take it off and put it on at will, so step out of it, roll it up and leave it hidden safely, ready for next time. You are always free to return to the ocean, to the child and the wise old one. They are with you. They are part of you, an expression of your own love and spiritual depth.

A prayer to end the meditation:

Dear God, you are the Great Mother and the Great Father of us all.
To us you entrusted the whole of this world, its oceans, its creatures, its plants,
the very rocks and soil beneath our feet. To us you entrusted the care of our brothers and
sisters, fathers and mothers in every land. When we walk this earth, let our steps be
light, let our eyes see beyond the wealth, to the vulnerability. Let us see beyond our greed
and need to the future, for the good of all. Dear God, open our eyes that we might see
in this world an expression of your love. May we hear the whisper of your voice
hovering even now, as in the beginning, over the waters of the deep,
and may we sense your spirit with us, in the heart of life. As we grow in your Spirit,
may we reach out to others, as ripples reach out from a stone thrown into a pool.
Father, may the meaning we seek ever deepen our love.
Amen

INTRODUCTION TO THE CONTEMPLATIONS

You may find that you prefer to dip into this next section rather than read it from beginning to end, but I shall explain its structure nevertheless.

There are seventy contemplations. The first contemplation recalls the sealskin, for this deals with our own identity. It addresses the very reason why we want to journey. Next is a human-made object, a door. This is a symbol of both barriers and opportunities, depending on how you see it, and is a word that occurs frequently in the New Testament. After that, to echo the soul's journey, I go to the pathway, symbol of the decisions we make about the direction of our lives. Much is said in Christian scripture about 'The Way'. Then comes a whole woodland of different trees. If we read the creation myth of Genesis, we find reference to the tree of life, and a tree bearing fruit of knowledge, of knowing good and evil, that sense of morality which sets us apart from the rest of nature. We can find much meaning wrapped up in the symbolism of the trees; indeed there is a whole tradition of tree lore and even a symbolic tree alphabet, ogham, associated with the Celts of the British Isles. After the trees come the creatures. You met Seal first, but here you may find the animal that came to you in the woods, or maybe some others. The Scriptures are rich in animal symbolism: the donkey, the sheep, terrifying sea monsters, the dove, to name but a few. People are animals, so some human dimensions feature here too.

Next come the natural features around us that, although they are not living as such, have a very real 'presence'. Here come the rocks (why did Jesus call Simon 'Peter'?), the water, mountains, the moon and sun. The Celtic Christians didn't perceive barriers between the natural and spiritual worlds like we tend to, so in this section too are spiritual presences such as angels. The final section brings us back to focus again on human-made things such as the axe, symbol of our power and responsibility; and altars, places of communion with God. Although in returning to the same theme we have come back to the beginning, we have also moved on from it, which is why I prefer to use the analogy of a spiral in my journeying rather than a circle. At the end is a personal statement of belief, a 'credo', reflecting the spirit of the whole book. Since we are all free to decide for ourselves what we believe, such attempts to consolidate our thoughts can prove interesting exercises.

The arena for my spiritual exploration is the world in which I live, my local trees, the creatures that come to my garden and those I see, or more often don't see, in the countryside I visit. Naturally, your own environment will shape your thoughts in a different way. There are no absolutes; the only necessity is to look for meaning and spiritual depth, seeing all with three eyes and a heart of love.

Each of the contemplations that follow is divided up for clarity's sake. Each begins with a biblical quotation chosen to reflect the spirit of the contemplation. Then come three sections. The first I have called 'Mind', being knowledge, intellect, rationality, reason and so on. Here I try to convey information and comments that might contribute to understanding. The second level I have called 'Body'; it is the realm of instinct, movement, gut-reaction, physical and emotional feelings, the childlike, emotional, even animal-like side to our personalities. Our bodies are integrally wrapped up with our emotions. Third is the level of spiritual insight, the part of us that has a sense that there is more than reason and instinct. This is the level of seeking deep meaning, of intuition, of prayer life. Here is the sense of 'something other'. These days we are all used to hearing about the importance of a holistic lifestyle; it is nothing new to state that each aspect – mind, body and spirit – is important in enjoying a balanced approach to life. I finish each contemplation with a prayer, a reminder that it is always God to whom we turn and return.

The Meditation Cards

At the back of the book, a set of seventy meditation cards have been included for your use. They correspond to the seventy contemplations and may be used within the context of group or individual meditation. They can be used in a variety of ways; below are some suggestions.

❖ Keep a card that seems pertinent to your current situation in your wallet or diary, or put it on a mirror or by a clock so that you are often reminded of that concept as you go about your daily life.

❖ Every morning, pick a card at random and read its related meditation. Use this as a theme for your day, seeking to deepen your own insight and develop your own thoughts on the symbol suggested.

❖ Lay out the cards face down and during meditation, whether alone or in a group, and pick one. Use the card you have selected as a focus for meditation. You may feel that the symbol you pick reflects thoughts and feelings already seeking expression in your mind. It may prompt you to gain a different perspective on a situation, or provide a vehicle for self-expression. This activity works better if all engaged in it have an opportunity to familiarise themselves with the seventy contemplations in advance. Time can be spent at the end, sharing thoughts on the cards chosen, and reading the contemplations contained in the book. These too can be used as the basis of group discussion and meditation, or individual reflection.

❖ Having read the contemplations, take time to lay out the cards on a table or the floor, grouping and rearranging them to find connections and relationships. You may find for example that you can make a link between several symbols that focus on self-development, on coping with difficulties, on responsibility, relationships, new beginnings, caring for others, the teachings of Jesus and so on, which you may then choose to single out and use as a set. Arranging the cards thus can be a way to clarify and order thoughts. You may find that you want to add new card symbols of your own.

❖ Become more deeply involved in individual symbols, adopting a card as your focus for a more prolonged search. My own contemplation of the symbol of a boat, for example, inspired me to take a course in sailing and canoeing, and then at the age of thirty to learn to swim. 'Boat' was my key symbol for several years! More recently, the many changes in my work situation, not all of which were pleasant, prompted me to meditate on (and under) the birch trees at the bottom of my garden. At that time I was in the habit of taking little birch twigs around with me, to remind me that I was glad to be making a new beginning!

❖ Become more deeply involved in the objects of the symbols themselves. Get to know all the native trees, not just from a book but by touching the bark and studying the leaves and twigs. Spend time with animals, learn to make pots, chop wood with an axe, light bonfires, listen to children, go for meditation walks through the woods, letting a prayer form in your mind for every squir-rel, stream and rock that you encounter. Live as though everything has a meaning, and you will enrich your own life. The cards can guide your way through, helping you to find a place to start.

Part 2

LEAVING NO STONE UNTURNED

'Listen! I am standing at the door, knocking; if you hear my voice and open the door,
I will come in to you and eat with you, and you with me.' (NRSV)
— Revelation 3:20. See also John 10:1–10, Song of Solomon 5:2

MIND: Food for thought

THE WORDS DOOR, OAK AND DRUID all seem to be related in the ancient languages of the British Isles (that is, in Welsh, Cornish and Scottish and Irish Gaelic). Doors are such an old invention they are easy to take for granted; yet, as human-made optional barriers, they demonstrate our need to create defences, define territories, keep the cold and enemies out and keep straying children and animals in. In John 10:1–10, Jesus talks about the importance of the gate on the sheepfold and goes on to say that he is the gate, or the door, and then that he is the shepherd. The claim is that he is the way to the realm of God, to safe, green pastures. We each have our own door, down some dusty corridor of our minds, placed there by ourselves to allow us to feel separate from God. We want to keep secrets; we are partly afraid that God will spoil our fun or interfere with our choices. But the writer of Psalm 139 reminds us, so poetically, that God cannot be shut out: 'Even before a word is on my tongue, O Lord, you know it completely. You hem me in, behind and before, and lay your hand upon me.' But perhaps the most evocative reference to a door in the Bible is in the Song of Solomon, where we might see the desire of the lovers as an allegory for the soul's longing for union with God.

BODY: What do you do?

❖ What is there in your life that you want to hide from God?

❖ What beliefs about God do you hold on to that frighten you?

❖ Do you hold on to childish beliefs and confusions bound up with your own relationship to your parents?

❖ No one yet has been able to describe God, so what kind of God would be most perfect to your mind?

❖ What does the door in your mind look like? A huge, heavy one, with locks and bolts? A garden gate? A little trapdoor in the roof? Where does it lead? How do you see your own 'green pastures'? How often do you go there?

SPIRIT: Meanings

THERE WAS NEVER A TIME when the Spirit in us became separate from the Spirit at the heart of God. The only part which is separate is that which is not lasting. In the realm of infinite Spirit, Spirit is all that there is. There is no separation, no barrier, no wall. In terms of our little human minds, there is struggling and pretence, fear and misunderstanding, but none of this is of the Spirit. That which is of the Spirit has always been there and will always be there, deep in the heart of love. Wanting to shut God out shows our misunderstanding of the loving nature of God. Trying to shut God out is as futile as Jonah's attempt to run away. Letting God in is letting joy, peace and love into our lives.

PRAYER

Open my soul door and enter, O my light, my joy.
Like flood waters through a sluice gate, rush in and fill me.
Though I sleep, my heart is awake, waiting for the sound of your steps at the door.

'Whoever follows me will never walk in darkness,
but will have the light of life.' (NIV)

— John 8:12. See also: Matthew 7:14, Psalm 56:13, 89:15, Isaiah 2:5, John 12:35

MIND: Food for thought

PATHWAYS LEAD US ON, but often diverge. We have to make a decision about which way to go next. They express the choice that we always have between the creative, positive way and the way of destruction; between the way of truth and that of dishonesty. Throughout history, religious thinkers from the Greek philosophers to the early church fathers have talked about 'two ways', equating life with light and walking in the presence of God, versus death, gloom and feelings of separation from God, even the presence of evil or malevolent forces. The earliest complete church liturgy known to scholars, the Didache, begins with a statement related closely to Plato's earlier writings: 'There are two ways, one of life, the other of death, and between the two ways there is a great difference.' The document goes on to describe the way of life as the following of the golden rule: to love God and our neighbours as we love ourselves, and to refrain from doing to others that which we would not want done to ourselves. Jesus and the early church both talked about 'The Way', one of the first names for the following of Jesus. In John 14:5, Jesus is recorded as stating that he is the way, the truth and the life; the way to the Father.

BODY: What do you do?

A TRACK BECOMES EASIER TO FOLLOW the more times it is walked along. The more often that we deliberately seek the narrow path, the easier it becomes for us to find it in the future. We do not have just one choice to make in our lives, we are constantly presented with choices. Sometimes we choose right, sometimes wrong, and then we need rescuing. Our journey through life is like following a map, knowing only where we start from. We decide where we are going, we decide which roads to use, we face the consequences of going the wrong way.

✤ In your own journey, who are your travelling companions? How do you feel about letting them go their own way?

✤ How do you make decisions?

✤ Who would you choose as your guide along the way?

SPIRIT: Meanings

W E CAN MAKE A DECISION to follow the way of Jesus, or not. At times it seems the hardest choice, especially when we are faced with a cross to bear. But Jesus never said it was easy to follow him, he said it was the way to find God. We have to want that with our whole heart to be able to keep to the path. How else can we resist the lures of wealth, prestige, power and material comfort? In the 'eyes of the world', it seems ridiculous to seek anything but material gain, yet for those who have glanced through the narrow gate, who have sensed that there is something other, a deeper and more wholesome path, then the lure of God's love grows stronger. It pulls us along, compelling us to keep on, until we reach the point where we know for sure that we are walking in the light of the Lord.

PRAYER

Father, guide me, Christ walk with me,
Holy Spirit lift me up that I may see the way ahead.

'Those who know your name will trust in you, for you, Lord,
have never forsaken those who seek you.' (NIV)
— Psalm 9:10

MIND: Food for thought

SEALS SEEM CLUMSY and out of place on land, as though they don't really belong. Their grace and speed is appreciated only when they are seen in the water. The Scottish myth of the shape-changing selkies, sometimes seal and sometimes human, connects us to a distant past, a time in our pre-history when people identified much more closely with the animals. We can imagine a time when people believed they could enter into mystical relationships with the spirits of the creatures through trance, artistic representation and dance. We can imagine a time when meaning was sought and found in the animal kingdom, when spirituality was bound up with respect and gratitude for the lives of these beautiful creatures, and the physical world could be transcended. But the reality is that we are animals, and it is up to us how in-touch or out-of-touch with the rest of the living world we choose to be. We can find depth and meaning or we can find emptiness. The seals remind us of our real nature, both our potential to be clumsy and out-of-place and to be at one with the environment. It is important to discover the place where we really belong. But the moment of transition, of 'taking the plunge', requires a degree of courage, for in pursuing our seal-soul, we depart from the ways of the world. That decision to put on the sealskin and dive takes trust and hope, where others see foolishness. It takes confidence in the knowledge that true security does not come from material possessions or even relationships, but comes from sensing God within and around, everywhere, like water.

BODY: What do you do?

HAVE YOU EVER TRAPPED OTHERS, by luring them into an environment in which you know they will be restricted? Has someone done the same to you? How can you change the situation? Do you want to?

✤ Have you ever felt you don't belong, and blamed yourself for being 'different', rather than seeking a more suitable place to be?

✤ Have you ever felt a yearning for greater depth in your life, a feeling that you could get in touch with your own soul?

✤ Are you willing to put your yearning for God before all else? Are you ready to seek first the Kingdom of God?

✤ When have you faced the decision over whether to make a faith-dive or stay safe with what you know? How did you react? Are you glad now, or sorry?

SPIRIT: Meanings

THE SEAL REPRESENTS OUR SPIRITUAL NATURE. Water is a symbol of divine oneness and the seal's ability to glide and dive through even inhospitable seas provides an analogy of the soul's freedom to explore spiritual depths. Henry Vaughan, the metaphysical poet, said, 'There is in God, some say, a deep but dazzling darkness.' It is the seal nature that dives down and down in search of that womb-dark peace. Here is our search for the truth that will set us free, the wisdom at our source, our mystical communion with God, that which we continuously yearn for. Until we find this 'place', our own desired haven, we continue to feel awkward and uncomfortable, frustrated in our efforts and unsure of our purpose. There are times when we have the opportunity to make that leap, that faith-full dive that seems so ridiculous and risky in the eyes of the world. Once we have made the dive for the first time, we will never look back.

PRAYER

Father of the Ocean, your depth is infinite, your mysteries profound.
I would put on the sacred robe of my sealskin and dive into your limitless arms.
I would explore the wonder of your world, at one with the flowing waters;
I would become again the creature that I was always meant to be,
at home in the depth of your eternal kingdom.

THE PLANT KINGDOM

'If you had known what these words mean, "I desire mercy not sacrifice,"
you would not have condemned the innocent.' (NIV)
— Matthew 12:7, quoting from Hosea 6:6

MIND: Food for thought

THE ANCIENT IRISH NAME FOR ALDER, *fearn*, appears to be related to the Irish word for man, perhaps because alder wood when cut turns a blood-like reddish orange. The tree thus became associated with the blood of Christ and was held to be sacred. Although Jesus's death was interpreted by first-century believers as a sacrifice in the manner of Temple sacrifices, it appears that Jesus's own view of God was influenced by the quotation from the prophet Hosea, 'I desire mercy not sacrifice,' which he is recorded to have used twice (Matthew 9:13 and Matthew 12:7). It is not clear whether Jesus saw his death as a sacrifice, although a glance at Luke 13:34 and its parallel in Matthew (23:37) implies that he saw death as the inevitable end for prophets who came to Jerusalem. Whatever our theological interpretation of the death of Jesus, the fact remains that he was a real man who died a horrible death, having stirred up the establishment's fury. Jesus at the last supper knew he was about to die and made the association between red wine and his blood. The drinking of the wine was to be in remembrance of him, but also, somehow, to mix his life with ours.

BODY: What do you do?

CHRIST'S BLOOD WAS SHED by cruel, misguided people. We know innocent blood is still shed, every day. Jesus died for a purpose: he showed a way through to God's kingdom. But others die and suffer for no purpose. We cannot share the blood of Christ without thinking of Matthew 25:31–46, '… I was hungry and you gave me no food, … sick and in prison and you did not visit me.' What we do to the least of God's children we do to Christ.

✤ Christ's blood was a sign of his humanity. When do you reach out in compassion to the Christ in others? When do you turn away?

✤ When do you support acts of cruelty and injustice by your silence, or your willingness to follow the crowd?

SPIRIT: Meanings

WE NEED TO REALISE the human element of God, that there is a Spirit of Love able to reach out through the sensitive souls around us. We need to accept the possibility that God is not remote, but within each of us, reaching out, bringing us hope in our moments of misery. Even Christ, in his last hours before death, wanted so much the presence of his followers, to have them with him as he waited for the inevitable to happen. But instead, sweating blood, he touched the deepest desolation of betrayal even by those who professed to love him most. He, the supreme embodiment of the Divine, uttered the seemingly final and dreadful cry, 'My God, my God, why have you forsaken me?' If Christ doesn't understand us in our loneliness and fear, then who does? And yet Jesus was not forsaken, he was brought back to the heart of God; therein lies our hope.

PRAYER

Brother of mine, walk with me. Friend of mine, talk with me.
From the courage of your love may I learn. On the strength of your love may I lean.
In the power of your love may I trust.
Through the endurance of your love may I find the true Way,
blessed brother of mine, Son of God.

'It is well with those who deal generously and lend,
who conduct their affairs with justice.' (NRSV)
— Psalms 112:5

MIND: Food for thought

THE APPLE TREE is representative of all fruit-bearing trees, prized so highly in the past that in several cultures, including that of the Old Testament, severe penalties were meted to those who wilfully caused damage. It represents all that is generous in nature and thus the quality of generosity itself. It represents the abundance and fertility of the earth, the wonder of the life cycle, the gratitude of harvest time. The apple tree is bound, along with the other crops on which we depend, to the ancient celebrations and ceremonies of an agricultural lifestyle. It is accessible to us, easy to harvest, easy to manage, easy to climb up and sit in. If you put your ear to the swaying branch of an orchard tree on a windy day, you will hear music carried down from the twigs as they rattle together, like the muffled tune of a xylophone. Apple gives; it seems to like us. Even in dying the tree gives, for its timber is so strong it is highly prized. It was rated even above hornbeam wood by millers, for making the cogs that turned the mill stones; apple was there at the heart of the machinery for giving the people their daily bread.

BODY: What do you do?

THE APPLE TREE IS A SYMBOL of the warm relationship that is possible between the natural world and ourselves. We can learn generosity from the fruit trees; our apples can be money, refuge, possessions, skills, time, a listening ear, but most of all, love. But it is not just people who should receive kindness; the earth gives to us constantly. What do we do in return? A parable in Luke's Gospel (13:1–9) describes a man who persuades the owner of a non-productive fig tree to give it another year's grace rather than fell it, in which time he will tend it carefully. The gardener understands that he is more likely to get results if he looks after the tree.

✤ Do you show genuine appreciation for those who give to you?

✤ Do you actively nurture the earth?

✤ How do you feel when you make a gift?

SPIRIT: Meanings

WE CAN IMAGINE OURSELVES as the little boy in the Gospel of John (6:1–14) who brings forward his picnic to share with the crowd and is met with adult cynicism: 'What good is this among so many?' If our gifts are not valued it is easy for us to feel hurt and, over time, bitter and drained. But Jesus took the child's gift and blessed it. He valued the child. In so doing, the gift somehow increased in value so that all could be nourished. Similarly, Christ noticed the true value of the poor widow's gift in the temple. He knew the cost of giving all. To Jesus, generosity meant giving his life, first in a ministry of healing and teaching and then in his death. He held nothing back, and thus gained everything. With gifts in mind I think of John 14:27: 'Peace I leave with you; my peace I give to you. I do not give to you as the world gives. Do not let your hearts be troubled, and do not let them be afraid.'

PRAYER

As my gratitude grows, so let my generosity grow too;
generosity to speak kindly and forgive freely,
to give gladly, offering good fruit from my heart,
nourished by the warmth of your peace.

'Let love and faithfulness never leave you; bind them around your neck,
write them on the tablet of your heart.' (NIV)
— Proverbs 3:3

MIND: Food for thought

THE MYTHOLOGICAL YGGDRASIL, sacred world-tree of the Vikings, was an ash, on which Odin hung for many days and nights before receiving the mystery of the runes. We might make a connection between the tree on which Odin gained the knowledge necessary for writing to develop, and the tree of knowledge mentioned in Genesis. The latter tree, though, had fruits which were not meant to be eaten, lest people in appreciating the difference between good and evil gained divine power. Ash can thus represent the mystical value of revealed knowledge, the authority a written text can convey, but also our need to study and gain understanding, for we do have the knowledge of good and evil. Our words, our writing, need to be infused with the responsibility that accompanies moral knowledge. When misuse of scripture is used to justify mismanagement of a nation or religion, then a whole people are oppressed and prevented from applying their critical faculties. It does not create a religious society but an anathema. The written word allows communication of meaning, which in turn enhances spiritual contemplation, but we need to be wary of turning any text into our only source of understanding and reasoning. Any book that we take as our guide through life must be qualified by the fact that life itself should be our guide and source of wisdom, for God is deep in the heart of life.

BODY: What do you do?

WE ARE ALLOWED TO QUESTION what we read. If it is true it will withstand our questioning. While we need to approach the written word in a spirit of humility, never assuming that our own wisdom is complete, we must also read with discernment and open-mindedness. We all read different nuances into the passages of our scriptures, depending on our own experience and our own hearts.

❖ What is your approach to newspapers? Which flavour of 'the truth' do you prefer?

❖ For you to believe what you read, what criteria does it have to meet? Does it have to be what you want to hear? Do you cross-check? Do you trust the integrity of some writers over others?

❖ Are you ever in the position where your writing has a direct impact on others?

❖ I once read an article entitled 'You are what you read'. What is your considered reaction to this statement?

SPIRIT: Meanings

LONG AGO, a wise soul walked into a beautiful garden rich with colour and life. So moved was this soul, and so sure of the presence of God, that s/he felt compelled to preserve part of that experience to give to others. Thus, picking a petal here and a flower or leaf there, a sample of the garden was lovingly pressed between the pages of a book. Now, if you open that book you will find those petals, and they will move you too, perhaps even give you a glimmer of God's presence with you, God's message for you. But the garden is still there, so why not experience it for yourself? Maybe you can add your own petals to the collection. Those who are truly inspired live their experience of God; the words they write are a by-product, an attempt to give that experience to others. By reading their words, we can be inspired in our own right. Beauty and inspiration, courage and the knowledge of God's will did not exist only in the past, only in a book. The garden is there for us all to enjoy.

PRAYER

Lord of Life, what books and what learning do little children have,
yet what wonder do they find in your world?
Let my books and my learning lead me to that same wonder and delight.
Save me from twisting and distorting words to suit my own ends.

'Ask and it will be given you; search, and you will find; knock and the door will be opened for you. For everyone who asks receives, and everyone who searches finds, and for everyone who knocks, the door will be opened.' — Matthew 7:7 (NRSV)

MIND: Food for thought

BEECH IS A TREE of immense beauty, a living cathedral. Its snake-like roots, which are often partly visible, and the sun-dappled leaf canopy reaching wide and high into the sky draw together the realms of heaven and earth. This is a tree singing of spiritual experience, a bridge between everyday life and the infinite realm of living love, between earth and heaven. Although Beech arrived in the British Isles later than many other deciduous trees, it still found its way into the ancient tree 'alphabet', ogham. Lines crossing a main stem form most characters, but the mark many now associate with beech resembles the curl of a shepherd's crook. The crook in itself is a powerful symbol, representing firm but caring guidance, the blessings of devoted leadership. Beech is thus associated with the role of the shepherd or pastor; here we can go when we feel lost, unsure of our way and in need of reassurance. The mere presence of a beech tree is uplifting, but through the symbol of the crook we can feel a deeper assurance that dynamic help is available. This is not a glib reminder of the strength we can find through pursuing a spiritual life, but an assurance that Spirit is interactive, and speaks through whatever channels we are prepared to listen to. Beech represents the promise that if we ask we are answered.

BODY: What do you do?

GUIDANCE CAN COME in many ways. A book may fall open at a particular place. A friend might call out of the blue; we might hear lyrics on the radio or a passage from a sacred text. A child might ask a question; we might speak with a stranger. As long as we are receptive and believe in the possibility of guidance, then it will come. It is not a tangible 'thing' that we can deliberately select. We cannot define the boundaries for ourselves and expect a clear answer. We need to be open, for the Spirit is free and blows where it will, like the wind. Sometimes it will surprise us. To try to bind the Spirit can only limit our spiritual experience. It sometimes takes courage to step beyond our usual sources of inspiration, but to do so is like throwing open the windows.

❖ What would you ask God?
❖ Do you feel God speaks to you in the Bible? Have you ever felt God speaking to you in some other way?
❖ What is your response to people who appear to be spiritually misguided?

SPIRIT: Meanings

THE MESSAGE OF CAUTION contained within beech is discernment. Many profess to speak with God as though they have a direct hotline; many more have written and spoken of their own convictions with such force that people are carried along by them like a great wave. There is a measure by which to determine whether a voice, a text, a thought is of God and is therefore to be trusted. That message must reverberate with love, with compassion, with a feeling of acceptance and warmth, with the healing of forgiveness and the perpetual chance to start again. It must vibrate with positive, joyful, creative energy; it must glow with a light and a delight of its own. It must affirm the worth of all, the presence of Spirit in the world, the radiant beauty of life. It also needs to feel right, it needs to strike a true chord in us. For there is no place in God for any malevolence; the Spirit is wholly good, the Greatest Good. To state anything less than this is simply to demonstrate human confusion and fear. Beech links earth and heaven like a bridge or a telephone cable. It is an assurance that we will receive insight and spiritual experience if our hearts and minds are open to the possibility.

PRAYER

Shepherd King, it is not that you are silent but that I fail to hear.
Make me listen to you, great guardian of my soul.

'But when the kindness and love of God our Saviour appeared, he saved us, not because of righteous things we had done, but because of his mercy. He saved us through the washing of rebirth and renewal by the Holy Spirit ...' — Titus 3:4 (NIV)

MIND: Food for thought

THE SILVER BIRCH TREE IS RICH IN SYMBOLISM. In many northern countries birch is the first deciduous tree to wake after the winter and since ancient times has represented renewal and new beginnings, a time of rejoicing after the long winter months. It is also the source of the traditional and very effective besom and is hence a symbol of sweeping clean and restoring order. The birch tree sheds parts of itself almost constantly, whether catkins, leaves, twigs or seeds. It is therefore a symbol of letting go of the past, and all that we no longer need. It represents an uncluttered physical and mental lifestyle. While birch seems slight and insubstantial in its beauty, it has great endurance, and its seeds travel far. Birch, to me, says 'metanoia', usually translated as 'repentance', but less esoterically, 'change of heart'. This was the call of Jesus and John the Baptist before him: to turn over a new leaf, to be ready for the kingdom or authority of God. A clean slate is the prerequisite of acceptance into the realm of heaven. Birch tells us that we can make this change over and over again, after every one of our spiritual winters. We can start again as often as we need to, not just once.

BODY: What do you do?

WE EACH HAVE TO DECIDE for ourselves what needs to be released and when, so that we have a clean slate to work on. There needs to be balance between holding on to what is of lasting value and discarding that which is out of date and unwholesome.

♣ What do you need to do to release the memories and emotions that hold you in the past?

♣ Do you see new beginnings as an opportunity to feel God working in your life, or as tests of your own strength and endurance? In which do you have more confidence?

SPIRIT: Meanings

IN ANY AND EVERY SITUATION we can choose to establish order and cleanliness or we can allow chaos and degeneration to take hold. The birch besom is a symbol of active cleansing. It is a symbol to demonstrate control over our own minds as we work on the side of anti-chaos. Silver birch is a tree of quiet self-confidence, of taking the lead in a subtle, almost inconspicuous way. In emptying ourselves ready for a new start, we open ourselves to the in-pouring of Spirit. A new start in Christ is an acceptance of a power greater than ours, a whole new approach to life. Instead of our old ways, we can be filled with love. Our spring waking is a waking to the presence of God.

PRAYER

Lord of Life, in you I find renewal.
Lord of Love, in you I find release.
Lord of Grace, in you I find forgiveness,
that the old may die in peace
and the new spring shoots
break through the sun-healed earth.

'Therefore do not worry about tomorrow, for tomorrow will worry about itself.
Each day has enough trouble of its own.' (NIV)
— Matthew 6:34. See also Luke 12:27, Matthew 6:28

MIND: Food for thought

A N EXTENSIVE SYMBOLISM of flowers evolved between medieval and Victorian times, referred to by writers including Shakespeare, and depicted by artists such as Botticelli. A careful look at the painting 'Birth of Venus' for example reveals daisies intricately painted onto the robe the goddess is about to be enveloped in. Daisies have long been associated with childhood and innocence. A tradition thought to date back several thousand years claims that the departed spirits of little children cause the flowers to grow. The name daisy comes from two words, day's eye, and refers to the way the flower-head responds to light: the petals open in sunshine and close in dull weather or darkness. While unhelpful in predicting future weather patterns, the daisy simply reflects the present situation. It can thus become a symbol of immediacy, of living in the present and responding only to the light or lack of light at that moment. Its connection with children is quite appropriate, since most children whose innocence is intact do have a tremendous capacity for living in the present, a gift valued by Jesus himself as the above quotation shows. In the sermon on the mount Jesus is quoted as using 'lilies of the field' to illustrate his teaching on living in the moment without worry. Perhaps if he had been speaking in Britain rather than Galilee he would have used daisies instead.

BODY: What do you do?

I T IS POSSIBLE to live virtually every moment in a kind of 'zombie' state, not fully 'here', because we are dwelling on something that has either gone or is yet to come. It is something we learn to do as we move from carefree childhood into care-full adulthood. Children who are not care-free share the trait of being not altogether 'with us', and their consequent lack of spontaneity and delight is one of the warning signs that something is amiss.

❖ At what point did you move from care-free to care-full?

❖ What can you do about your adult cares that would contain them more tidily into the time in which they belong?

❖ How do you respond to the words of Jesus recorded in Matthew 11:28, 'Come to me, all who are weary and burdened, and I will give you rest'?

SPIRIT: Meanings

D AISIES ARE A REMINDER to us that it is the present moment that belongs to us most truly; every moment is a chance to change, to experience joy, to learn. Living in the present also allows us to bless every moment. I feel differently about cooking dinner, for example, when I am appreciating and giving thanks for every ingredient as it is prepared and added, than when I am using the time alone in the kitchen to worry over some bugbear. Yet authentic bugbears are imaginary creatures conjured up to intimidate children into conformity. As adults we give ourselves nightmares, but are the worries any more real? If we are to follow Jesus's advice we are to let them go, imaginary or not, for they prevent us from appreciating the only real time that we have, time that should be spent in the presence of God.

PRAYER

Father, in this brief moment in time,
let me see the world around me with gladness and delight,
let me find fascination in small things,
let me set my worries free like a child's balloon,
let me laugh as they float away on a cloud.
Now, I take a breath and release a breath, I and the rest of life.
We breathe together, we share the air, we share this moment.
We are all your little children and all that we need, you give.

'Beloved, let us love one another, because love is from God;
everyone who loves is born of God and knows God.' (NRSV)
— From 1 John 4:7–21

MIND: Food for thought

HAWTHORN, with its abundance of frothy-white, heavily scented springtime blossoms, was traditionally associated with the female and with spring celebrations. At one level, it was a tree to represent youthful delight in first love. At another level, hawthorn was associated with the wise old woman who sits and weaves, knowing the patterns of life from ancient times. Respected, at times feared, she was sometimes said to be the gatekeeper of the other world of spirit, sitting as she did in her death-bed vigils. She it is who eases our passage through life. This venerable grandmother, like a fairy godmother, represents the touch of God, the miracle worker who takes mere chance and twists it into opportunity, spinning strong threads from the wisps and scraps gleaned from along the wayside. It is she who dips into the cauldron of chaos and ladles out warm nourishment, who sits with us in our labour pains and with strong but gentle hands draws forth life from the blood and tears. She it is who has the keys of hope for humanity, the wisdom of years, the kindly authority of the midwife, the compassion of the healer, the insight of one who has nursed the dying and glimpsed beyond.

BODY: What do you do?

LEARNING TO LOVE is not always easy. There are thorns on the hawthorn just as there are on the rose, that other timeless symbol of love. While some people give us something in return, such as comfort, security, excitement or self-esteem, others don't. We might find them repulsive, irritating, offensive, aggressive, and it is difficult to set judgements aside. It is difficult to remember that every soul is a brother or sister, and each has their own reason for becoming the way they are. Jesus showed his compassionate love for all, however repulsive; he was even willing to touch lepers.

❧ Who do you love least in the world? Why? If you were to pray for that person, what would you say? Try it!

❧ Whom do you find it easiest to love? Why? Pray for that person too!

SPIRIT: Meanings

AS WE BEGIN TO FIND LOVE in those around us, it is as though a new world is unfolding. We enter a realm where suddenly each being seems like an angel (albeit one with amnesia), whether an angel of teaching, or of blessing or of guidance. Each being that we meet brings with them a lesson of God's love for us to learn, thus every person, every living thing, becomes an object of gratitude. Our task is to learn to love with the love of God, for in so doing we are part of God. To love unconditionally and unselfishly, from the depth of our spiritual strength, is to bring heaven to earth within ourselves. But heaven, like the Spirit of God, cannot be bound. Once it has found a home it will shine out from there like light through a window, that all may be drawn towards the comfort, out of the dark, cold night, like children drawn to the welcoming hearth fire of old Grandmother Hawthorn. God's love is unconditional. That is what we too have to work towards.

PRAYER

Loving Grandmother God,
in my sickness you have nursed me, in my labour pains you have held me,
in my death you will watch as my soul finds freedom.
May I learn to love without discrimination,
may I learn to love all as sleeping angels of heaven.

'Holy Father, protect them in your name that you have given me, so that they may be one as we are one. While I was with them I protected them in your name...' (NRSV)
— John 17:11–12. See also Psalm 16:1, Psalm 32:7

MIND: Food for thought

HOLLY IS THE OBVIOUS SYMBOL of protection and defence. It holds its fruit dear and only allows access to selected creatures, small enough to avoid the prickles. Holly is also a symbol of life in the depths of winter, a sign of hope in adversity. On the physical level, holly makes a safe refuge, a great comfort when we feel vulnerable and weak. Holly is a tree that asserts its own space and does not allow intrusion. At the mental and emotional level, holly, again, is a symbol of assertiveness, of maintaining autonomy. Jesus talked about the vulnerability of his followers; he was under no illusion that their lives would be safe, yet he looked beyond the fear caused by physical attack, exhorting his followers not to be afraid of those who can kill the body 'and after that can do nothing more'. Such courage takes great conviction that there is something 'other', some higher purpose to life, some reason why in dying all is not lost. At his trial, Jesus offered no defence, he saw no need. He suffered, yet he saw through the agony. In our own spiritual winters, when all seems bleak and hostile, we might take heart at the sight of holly, still very much alive.

BODY: What do you do?

UNLIKE JESUS, most of us on Earth are still learning to feel a constant sense of oneness with the Spirit of God. It is our newness, our fragility, which needs protecting; in our spiritual rebirth we are like butterflies emerging from a cocoon, delicate and at first helpless, waiting for strength in our wings.

❖ When you feel vulnerable, which part of you is reacting? Your intellect? Your instinct? Your inner child? Your physical body? What can you do to help yourself to feel safe? Have you asked for help?

❖ Christ prayed to God for our protection; he wanted to look after us. How can you offer protection to those who are are weak or vulnerable?

❖ Do you feel that there is a higher purpose to life? How do you respond to Christ's defiance of death?

SPIRIT: Meanings

WHILE WE MIGHT WELL TAKE TRIALS, temptations and tribulations, we are reassured by Paul's words in 1 Corinthians 10:13, speaking to Christians at risk of real persecution for their faith: 'God is faithful, and he will not let you be tested beyond your strength, but with the testing he will also provide the way out so that you may be able to endure it.' At times when even the spirit within us cries out in despair, we must hold on to our own confidence in God. That is what must be protected at all costs, for if we lose hold of our spiritual strength, if we let the horrors of the world and of physical attack sweep away our sense of God within us, then we can sink only deeper and deeper into fear and isolation. It is fear that breeds hate and it is hate that refuses to permit healing. We must hold on, like a child clutching a kite string, for our sense of God's love is the root of sanity, of wisdom and of hope.

PRAYER

Holy Father,
give me the confidence of your presence,
that I may walk boldly and in peace.
Encircle me with your power, encircle the world with peace.

'… Whoever wishes to become great among you must be your servant, and whoever wishes to be first among you must be the slave of all.' (NRSV)
— Mark 10:43. See also Matthew 20:20, John 13

MIND: Food for thought

HORNBEAM IS A TREE of striking contrasts. It can grow to massive size with a rough, twisted trunk, but bears the most delicate, finely veined leaves. It is a living demonstration of accepting the rough with the smooth. Hornbeam wood has immense strength; it used to be turned into cartwheel and waterwheel axle bearings, being able to take the wear and strain so well. It is also used for piano hammers and chopping boards. While its functions may seem modest compared to the beautiful buildings and fleets of ships built of oak, through its durability hornbeam is and was a facilitator, enabling people to meet their needs. Hornbeam is thus a reminder of humility. It teaches that not only are the great among us sometimes required to do apparently lowly tasks, but also that some of these so-called lowly tasks actually require great strength. This is the tree to represent the act of Jesus washing his disciples' feet, the image of a master showing his humble equality with those who have learned all he has to teach. It also reflects the sentiment expressed by Jesus in response to James and John's request to share Jesus's power. Jesus does not think in terms of human power and glory, but in closeness to God.

BODY: What do you do?

HORNBEAM IS THE TREE for getting hands dirty, for taking action in unromantic, unglamorous and sometimes small ways that can actually make a big difference to the lives of real people.

❖ Jesus touched 'unclean' lepers, 'demoniacs', diseased women, corpses; he shared meals with despised prostitutes and corrupt tax collectors, and gave most of his time to the poor, uneducated people of the villages. If Jesus were here today, whom would he be spending his time serving?

❖ How aware are you of the squalor and poverty around you? Where do the local homeless go at night? How many children have no socks in the winter and no hot meal? How many live in homes with no furniture, heating or toys? What about local care of the elderly? Have you ever lived on the equivalent of a pension?

❖ What ways of serving are open to you?

SPIRIT: Meanings

SERVICE TO OTHERS is often interpreted as a form of self-sacrifice, which is particularly apt to hornbeam, with its widespread use in butchers' blocks. Christian congregations pray that they might be 'a living sacrifice', working in service to the will of God. The ultimate sacrifice however, the laying down of life for the sake of another, in heroic self-disregard, is felt to have been made in the death of Jesus. Our living sacrifices should honour the memory of those courageous enough to die for the sake of others; our actions should mean that such lives were not lost in vain. Jesus went to the unlovely and loved them, and in the end he died for them, his 'little children'. His ministry demonstrated that all are acceptable to God. He did not just serve the deserving poor so loved by Victorian do-gooders; he found the real rejects, the lowest of the low, and brought them to God's kingdom.

PRAYER

Lord Jesus, who took the bowl from a servant
and knelt before your own disciples,
teach me the meaning of true nobility;
teach me to respect
the worth and dignity of all.

*'A leper came to him begging him, and kneeling he said to him, "If you choose,
you can make me clean." Moved with pity, Jesus stretched out his hand and touched him,
and said to him, "I do choose. Be made clean!" ' — Mark 1:40–41 (NRSV)*

MIND: Food for thought

LAVENDER is such a popular herb it represents our innate understanding of the connection between a soothed mind and a healed body. The quest for health has inevitably preoccupied us since prehistory, and in the process people have subjected themselves to a spectrum of treatments. It is widely accepted now that true healing is often more than a matter of mechanics: a person's state of mind can have repercussions on their body. But this, of course, is not a new idea; much faith is placed by many in the ancient oriental healing arts, likewise the philosophies in which they are rooted. Our search for holistic health can lead us into an exploration of ancient spirituality. It can also lead to a superficial impression of very deep wisdom, and conversely, great trust in misguided theories and practitioners. Jesus, living in a time when surgery was likely to kill, and many diseases were dealt with through religious rituals, made the link between fear, guilt and sickness and, conversely, the connection between peace of mind and health. His technique reflected the urgency of his mission: it required immediate change; the children of God had to be made whole. The tradition of healing continued in the early Church through the laying-on of hands.

BODY: What do you do?

❖ Trace the accounts of healings by Jesus and his followers. What do you make of them?

❖ Have you had experience of Christian laying-on of hands? Would you try it? Do you think it can only be counted a success if the specific symptom disappears?

❖ Do you ever look for a psychological root to your illness? Do you think feelings of fear, anxiety, rejection, guilt and worthlessness ever play a part?

❖ You may find meditation helpful in times of illness. You might close your eyes and imagine the presence of Jesus, laying his hand on you. You might sense his love, his wish for you to feel peace. You might talk to him about what hurts, both in your body and in your feelings. Tell him your fears, know that you are always accepted by him, that his compassion reaches out even now. If you fear for someone else who is ill, then imagine Jesus with them, and tell him what your feelings are.

SPIRIT: Meanings

JESUS WANTED PEOPLE TO BE WELL; healings were a sign of God's closeness and love. Many of the illnesses Jesus is reported to have healed, such as leprosy, excluded the sufferer, making them ritually 'unclean'. By healing, Jesus was making it possible for desperate people to feel included again, to be free from the worry of poverty, of failing their families and of punishment from God. By touching a leper, he showed that he placed that person's well-being above his own 'cleanliness'. He gave lepers a passport back into the community, to get on with their lives. The quotation above describes Jesus's deep sense of compassion. We must hold on to this love, and to the knowledge that he wanted us to find peace of mind, and freedom from worry and guilt. In our suffering, this can be the hardest thing to find. We should not be angry with ourselves for our inadequate faith, nor with Jesus for failing us. But we should try to be open to change, starting from the inside with our own feelings. Take ownership of the words in John 14:27. 'Peace I leave with you, my peace I give to you. I do not give to you as the world gives. Do not let your hearts be troubled, and do not let them be afraid.'

PRAYER

Lord, renew a right spirit within me, so that I may see with the inner eye of wisdom. Then, I shall see my sickness from within, and so too might my inner healing begin, first with the growing sense of your peace. As I seek to heal the troubles of my mind, let me be ready for the changes your love can bring.

'And Joshua recorded these things in the Book of the Law of God. Then he took a large stone and set it up under the oak near the holy place of the Lord.' (NIV)

— Joshua 24:26. See also Genesis 35:4

MIND: Food for thought

I N FOLKLORE, oak is a tree of power, resonating with warm, deep, mirthful love. Oak is host to more life than any other British tree and has room in its wide arms for all the passion, the joy and the pain of life; it is a tree of wholeheartedness and supportive love. It is also a tree of ancient veneration. It is believed that in pre-Roman times oak was the most holy tree of the druids. Oak has been with us throughout the growth of our spirituality. It has seen the pagan days of blood, light, dark and earth, the nature spirit gods and goddesses, the sacred groves and ancestral tombs, then the missionary work of the early saints who would teach under its shade. After them came the sects formed over centuries as people struggled to express their own religious understanding, sometimes suffering terribly as a result. Oak holds a remnant of our past, a precious fragment that was suppressed out of fear and misunderstanding but now needs to grow back. Oak is our link with the part of our culture that loved the natural world, respected it, found sanctity in it and drew from it all meaning to walk wisely through life. If we are looking for life, then oak should hold a lesson for us: all nature knows there is a home to be found in the boughs or the roots and there is shelter beneath the generous canopy. The oaks of the Holy Land saw a similar history: Genesis 35:4 describes how the people gave up their old idols and buried them under the oak at Shechem, as a sign of new loyalty to the one true God. The quotation above records the time when the Children of Israel renewed their promise of faithfulness to God. The stone placed under the same old oak was a witness to their vow.

BODY: What do you do?

THE SPIRIT OF OAK is still with us now, in our age of materialism, waiting with wide arms outstretched for the few who know something is missing from modern life, who wander away from the crowd, up into the woods to find light and life and peace. This is the point at which we realise there is nothing new under the sun and even we have no surprises for God. We can stop worrying and let ourselves be accepted, 'warts an' all', by the One who has seen it all before.

❧ What idols can you bury as a sign that you are renewing your faithfulness to God?

❧ What aspects of your personality do you think are hardest to accept? God accepts them.

❧ Whom do you struggle to accept and why?

SPIRIT: Meanings

ASSOCIATED WITH STRENGTH and durability, oak is like a kind grandparent who sees everything, blames no one and blesses all. Under oak, we can be children again, safe and free to be lost in the beautiful moment, wrapped up in our own loves and wondering. Oak represents the God who accepts our humanity, our longings and desires, our hunger and desperation, and, as one who has lived a long and wise life, knows the subtlety and depth of human emotion. Oak can remind us of the ministry of Jesus, who deliberately went to people who felt they were rejected by society, and told them they were accepted by God. Even tax-collectors and prostitutes were welcomed, and it came as a shock to the religious establishment to hear Jesus state that such people were entering the Kingdom of Heaven ahead of the 'righteous'. Nobody is perfect yet all are loved by God. That is the good news of oak.

PRAYER

Loving Grandfather God,
thank you that despite my imperfection,
you welcome me into your infinite presence.

'He cut down cedars, or perhaps took a cypress or oak. He let it grow among the trees of the forest, or planted a pine, and the rain made it grow.' (NIV)
— Isaiah 44:14

MIND: Food for thought

THE PINE IS PRIZED among trees for its rapid, straight growth and its suitability for fuel and furniture. The ancient forests of Scotland remind us of the richness and variety of life that can be supported when conifers are allowed to grow naturally. It is an awe-inspiring thought to imagine a time following the last ice age, when such forests covered far more of the land. The landscape we are used to, while beautiful, has a shaved look about it, as smooth as a newly shorn sheep. The land has changed because our ancestors changed it. Fortunately, tastes are gradually changing too. Replanting has begun on an increasingly large scale in Europe. But our forests will always be small compared with the rainforests of warmer lands; we have to look beyond our own back yard to the wider environment. We have to be aware of the economic pressures that force people to destroy these unique habitats, as essential to the health of the planet as our own lungs are to our bodies. Closer to home, we can compare the vibrancy of naturally growing conifers with the plantations, which, while they serve their purpose as crops for easy harvesting, support very little life. Pine represents the magnificent ecosystem that grows naturally, if respected. All within the system interrelates, everything has a place, the food chain is in balance, and as old trees die, light touches the floor and lets new growth through. If people are to interfere, it needs to be in a way that enhances the life of the place, not just exploiting it and destroying the life within.

BODY: What do you do?

WE ARE COLLECTIVELY RESPONSIBLE for the health of the planet's ecosystems. Thoughtless demand for products results in over-harvesting of supplies, whether herbs for remedies, fish, cheap meat or hardwoods for garden furniture. Of course people who struggle to make a living will do whatever they can to survive, but we have seen the imbalance that results from communities becoming dependent on selling cash crops rather than concentrating on their own self-sufficiency. Our greed and ignorance can exacerbate poverty just as it can result in destruction of habitats.

❖ How much do you know about the origin of products you buy? How much do you know about the effects of western consumerism on the earth? What difference could you make?

❖ Do you have access to fair trade and genuine ecologically friendly products? Do you use them?

SPIRIT: Meanings

I REMEMBER GOING WITH A GROUP OF FRIENDS on a spiritual retreat, into an area of forest in Scotland. Our idea was to meditate there in the forest, to feel close to the life, and 'tune in' to the smells and sounds around us. I had been looking forward to the experience and was sure I would emerge with deeply enhanced spiritual vibes! But as I sat at the base of a great pine tree, I gradually felt overwhelmed by a sadness that I could not overcome, despite my resistance. I heard the birds and the stream, I smelled the fresh pine resin, I loved the place, but all I could think of was its vulnerability. I felt that I, a representative of the human race, was a hostile presence in that place of beauty, and that all I could do was ask forgiveness, on humanity's behalf. I wished I could be at one with the forest, but I sensed a huge gulf, created long ago. What can bridge that divide? The quotation above is from a passage ridiculing the fashioning of idols. We take the trees and use them selfishly and senselessly. Why?

PRAYER

Lord of the forests, Lord of life,
Let me walk lightly on the earth, taking no more than I really need. Let me always give
thanks, let me give back to the earth, whenever I take. I grieve that the human race has
harmed the earth; we have wounded our own mother. I grieve that the forests, were they
conscious, would mistrust our presence. Take away our hypocrisy, our double standards
and greed, and show us how to be ambassadors of harmony and life, that the woods and
forests might welcome our presence as healers, not fear us as destroyers.

'…till the Spirit is poured upon us from on high, and the desert becomes a fertile field, and the fertile field seems like a forest. Justice will dwell in the desert and righteousness live in the fertile field.' — Isaiah 32:15 (NIV)

MIND: Food for thought

IN FOLKLORE, rowan symbolises the sacred, a gateway to spiritual assistance in earthly life. Rowan is a symbol of reverence and wonder, awe at the beauty of the natural world and humility concerning that which lies beyond, of which we have so little knowledge. In ancient times the rowan was called many things including 'delight of the eye', and the 'tree of life'. Rowan is particularly remarkable in its ability to flourish in harsh conditions; it is not deterred by windswept mountainsides and rocky outcrops but stands out boldly, its roots twisting through rock crevices to find moisture. It does not seem diminished by its surroundings but gives inspiration and comforting warmth, whether on a city street or by a mountain stream. I became particularly drawn to rowan over the ten years I spent teaching in a difficult inner-city school. The whole environment seemed so bleak sometimes and I wanted so much for the school to be a place of light and inspiration for the children. I remember praying about the place, almost willing some angel to come and hover overhead. The next day I glanced at the little school garden and noticed as though for the first time a radiant rowan, bright with berries and autumn leaves, shining like a beacon of hope; a glorious symbol of spiritual presence and assistance, right in the middle of that harsh environment, and something beautiful to delight the children's eyes.

BODY: What do you do?

ROWAN ASKS NOT FOR CYNICISM but exploration. For in denying the possibility of a spiritual life, we might find we are depriving ourselves of an endless source of nourishment and strength. It is not a weakness to ask for help, there is nothing to lose in seeking out our guardian angels or guiding spirits. Feeling supported, feeling loved, we might feel our roots gripping a little more firmly in the life-bearing earth, so that we too, like the rowan tree, might take in the nourishment that is available to us, provided unceasingly by our nurturing Mother-Father God. Thus, we might come to shine out regardless of where we are or who we are with, simply because we have received the gifts that are there for us and have allowed them space to grow.

* What hostile environment do you know, where the spirit of rowan might take root?
* Have you ever felt drained, trying to bring light to a gloomy place? Could there be another source of power?

SPIRIT: Meanings

ROWAN IS A TREE long associated with the 'other' world of natural power, where there is freedom for angels or guardian spirits to stretch their wings. Rowan is a symbol of affirmation, of confidence in the presence of the Great Power of Creation, the infinite Love that wills for us to live and find love and in so doing return to that Love enriched. As adults, many of us grow cynical about the possibility of spiritual help, even spiritual development itself. In a world so full of uncertainties, where we seem so much in the dark, so alone in trying to work out what it's all about, it does not take much to become disillusioned, defensive, afraid and hostile. But in denying the spiritual, we cut off our own lifeline. It is not in the nature of Spirit to cause destruction or pain; it is the nature of Spirit to heal, to nurture and empower. In our bleakest hours and in the bleakest places, we may blame anything or anyone, but whatever the cause of misfortune, it will never be the source of Love.

PRAYER

Christ of the wilderness,
just as angels came and ministered to you in the desolation,
send out your angels to this barren and lonely place
that it might become a place where children laugh and play in happiness.

'... But as for what was sown on good soil, this is the one who hears the word and understands it, who indeed bears fruit and yields, in one case a hundredfold, in another sixty, and in another thirty.' — Matthew 13:23 (NRSV)

MIND: Food for thought

SEEDS ARE MENTIONED frequently in the writings of the Bible; wheat and barley were the staple diet of the inhabitants of the fertile crescent. The story of Joseph in Egypt, as manager of the grain silos, demonstrates the dependence on a good harvest. Many laws surrounded the harvesting of the grain, including the right of the poor to glean from the field, as we read in the book of Ruth. The more ancient people of the Bible were living at a time when many cultures worshipped deities associated with the grain. Worship showed awe at the property of the seeds to 'die' and then rise again with abundant new life, and there was a sense of gratitude towards 'Mother' earth, for providing nourishment and life. The Israelites would have shared this sense of awe, but were forbidden from worshipping the Canaanite fertility deities; they were to give all praise to God. But the wonder of seeds never left the people; for example, in Mark 4:27 we read of a man who sows seed and whether he sleeps or wakes, the seeds sprout 'though he does not know how'. In 1 Corinthians 15, Paul took up the pagan symbol of the dying and rising grain and used it as his own symbol of the resurrection body: 'What you sow does not come to life unless it dies.' Thus, we can find a wealth of imagery concerning seeds, but always bound to their capacity, despite smallness and apparent lack of life, to produce the most wonderful harvest.

BODY: What do you do?

WE CAN ASK OURSELVES what we create from our own hearts, what fears, hopes and joys do we sow around us. We might hope that our cerebral and metaphysical offspring should reflect grace and inner radiance, true celebration of life. When we realise that we seem to be falling short however, and that we are producing nothing but sterile, bitter berries, we should not despair. We are to be both active and passive, simultaneously a parent tree and the receptive earth.

❖ When the word of God falls on you, how well is it received? Are you fertile soil, or are you all brambles and stones?

❖ In what sense might accepting the word of God affect the quality of your own seeds or fruit?

❖ Take time to study the references to seeds, wheat and harvests in the Bible!

SPIRIT: Meanings

OUR THOUGHTS ARE LIKE SEEDS, carried wide by the wind. Our words sustain the ideas we give fruition to. A tree is known by its fruit, and in each fruit, good or bad, there are seeds that have the potential to increase either the goodness or the flaws of their parent tree. Yet the quotation above casts us as the earth, ready to receive a seed. Rather than sending forth our own 'power', we are asked to cultivate the qualities needed to be able to accept a greater power. Our receptivity determines the abundance of the yield, yet once sown God's seed will take root and grow within us. The same image is used in the parable of the mustard seed: if we have even the smallest glimmer of hope in God, it will grow. It is this faith, this receptivity to God, that bears the greater yield; when we rely solely on our own efforts we are always limited. We need to be concerned not just with our own fruit, but also with being receptive to the seed of God, and thus truly productive.

PRAYER

Lord of the Harvest, you who sow seeds in our hearts and wait for them to grow,
let me notice those seeds and tend them,
so that in my time I might produce seeds of my own that are worthy of your name.
As I wait for the harvest, let my confidence in you grow.

'See, I have chosen Bezalel son of Uri ... and I have filled him with the spirit of God,
with skill, ability and knowledge in all kinds of crafts ...' (NIV)
— Exodus 31:2–3

MIND: Food for thought

SYCAMORE is sometimes looked down on by British tree-lovers; it is not a native tree but was brought over from the continent relatively recently. For this reason it does not have a place in the ancient Celtic tree alphabet, ogham, and relatively little folklore is attached to it. But sycamore enjoys being here; it grows prolifically and has many uses, notably in violin-making and as smooth, pale boards for dance floors. Left to grow, sycamore reaches a majestic stature, and is colourful and shapely. The underside of the bark on a mature tree, if exposed, reveals growth ripples like wave patterns in damp sand, as though a river has been running inside the tree. Sycamore belongs with us now and deserves a place in our spiritual thinking. The tree's association with music and dance is inspiration in itself. Every culture has found its own sounds. Song, dance and music seem to be natural to humans. There is a mystical quality about the creation of sound, and a vast capacity to communicate on an emotional and spiritual level. Sycamore thus presents itself as a symbol of the creative arts, the ways in which we go beyond the normal activity of life to express ourselves.

BODY: What do you do?

SYCAMORE SYMBOLISES the bypassing of clumsy words, the transcending of the humdrum into humming and drumming. It is a celebration of the richness of human experience, from love to fury, ecstasy to despair. It is not only music through which we communicate the depths of our hearts and souls: sycamore extends itself to the whole world of creativity, to each and every way we find to bring what is hidden within into the open. The value of creativity cannot be underestimated. Through trying to paint or play our feelings, we study them, we look more deeply at ourselves and in so doing come to understand ourselves more deeply; it is a process of turning inside-out, of introspection, of the struggle to find not only beauty but meaning.

❖ How do you express yourself?

❖ Did negative comments in your childhood somehow dent your confidence? You need to exorcise those hurts and be free!

❖ In what ways are you captured by the spirit of creativity?

SPIRIT: Meanings

WITHIN EACH OF US there is a terrible primordial scream, an unearthly whoop of delight, an unquenchable, pulsating longing, a sweet, soft feeling of tingling excitement, a belly-laugh that has been locked up since the trailing away of our childhood. These feelings fester and stagnate if they are not aired. There is an indisputable connection between our mental well-being and our bodily well-being. Creation is a divine act; sound is an image of the creative power of God. In creating, we find a new energy, a passion, a driving need to create again. There is euphoria in true creativity that seems to be a direct line to the Spirit. Those held by the creative urge seem to shine with an excitement, an inner bubbling, a sense that they are communicating a part of the Truth, because what they are making is part of their own essence. To find this inner power is to find a door to self-understanding, to self-acceptance, and thus to self-healing. It is a door that we all need to find within ourselves.

PRAYER

Holy Spirit of God, inspire me to create works of beauty and depth,
free me to create works from within my own soul.
May all I do be to the glory of God.

*'By the rivers of Babylon – there we sat down and there we wept when
we remembered Zion. On the willows there we hung up our harps.
For there our captors asked us for songs …'* — Psalm 137:1–3 (NRSV)

MIND: Food for thought

WATER-LOVING WILLOW, in all its varieties, is distinctive for its flexible, whip-like branches. Several traditions connect the tree with sadness and loss: willow leaves used to be worn in Britain as a sign of mourning over lost loves and it is in the branches of willow trees that the Psalmist says the captive Jews hung their harps. There is a feeling of empathy with willow; it is a tree of quiet, comforting company, like the shoulder we sometimes wish for to cry on. Willow has many messages for us. It is not by chance that cricket bats are made of it, for the wood has a uniquely springy property – it is not so rigid that it snaps under impact. We could aim to be like a cricket bat when we receive a blow; we could deliberately cultivate the ability to deflect (psychological) missiles, like water off a duck's back. Willow rods can sprout independently if placed in the ground. When we feel cut off, then we too need to take the opportunity to grow again, if ever we find ourselves back 'down to earth'. Willow thus becomes a multifaceted symbol addressing our attitude to hardships. It helps us not only to cope, but to think about how we might cope better.

BODY: What do you do?

❖ How do you respond to the suggestion that, after the initial gut reaction, you choose whether to keep feelings that hurt you, or to let them go?

❖ Some things hurt us so much they sink in deeper than our conscious minds and stay with us a long time. Children bring their hurts into adulthood, adults repress hurts and put on a brave face. Yet there is much grief deep down in many people; there is a great weight that stops our expression of joy. Various schools of thought offer advice on how to cope with this fact. Some would seek to heal the inner child and go back to all the hurts, addressing each one. Others would prefer to make a break with the past; a clear decision to turn over a new leaf. Which approach seems right to you? Or is there another way?

SPIRIT: Meanings

NEXT TIME you feel sad or hurt, imagine a willow tree beside a river or, even better, go and sit under one. Imagine yourself as the tree. Loosen up a little and let yourself feel more supple, more flexible, more able to move with the wind. Stretch and relax your tired, tense muscles and allow for the possibility that you are not alone, that the ability to bounce back or grow new shoots is there within you. Look down at the water. You choose to live here, always in contact with that which unites all living things; the water is part of you; it cleanses you and soothes you. Notice the direction in which your river is flowing, onwards to meet the sea, always in that great cycle. See your sadness crystallising in one of the leaves, turning it yellow. It is ready to drop: let go your leaf, let it float down the river. Do the same again, until your autumn leaves fall like tears, carried away by the river, leaving you not empty, but ready to prepare for the spring. If you do not do this with your hurts, then they will continue to hurt you. Keeping them is like clutching a knife blade; you must let go or the wound will get deeper and deeper.

PRAYER

Loving Father, when our songs fail and our mirth dies,
when we can see only sadness, then let us come to the river and remember you.
Let us find that we can bend without breaking, we can take blows without cracking,
we can let go our grief without becoming any less in ourselves.

67

'... but those who drink from the water that I will give them will never be thirsty. The water that I will give will become in them a spring of water gushing up to eternal life.'
— John 4:14 (NRSV)

MIND: Food for thought

THE YEW IS AN ANCIENT SYMBOL of eternal life or survival after death. The atmosphere beneath a yew tree is comfortingly warm, dark and still; it is a place of earthy peace. It is no coincidence that old yew trees stand in many churchyards, like silent sources of the restfulness we wish upon those who have left us. Perhaps the most significant feature of the yew is its longevity, extended into perpetual life by the growth of daughter shoots which flourish around the mother tree as she gradually fades away. The shoots are of the same substance as the main tree and are connected by root systems. The presence of the yew remains, but in remaining multiplies, eventually shedding its age and fragility for a new, healthy form. Over centuries, yews form groves by spreading out like ripples from a splash. Instead of the finality of death and decay, yew demonstrates continuity and the expansion of life outwards, ever growing and reaching beyond itself. At root level, yew symbolises oneness, while its evergreen leaves are another symbol of everlasting life. Yew trees however are also poisonous. This poison represents that which we fear about death, the wariness in confronting our own feelings and beliefs, the distress caused by suffering and witnessing suffering in another. To think meaningfully and constructively about death, we need to have an equally meaningful insight into what life is really for.

BODY: What do you do?

Beliefs about a possible afterlife are of critical importance in spiritual thinking, because they determine what we believe about God.

❖ What thoughts did you have about an afterlife as a child? How have these thoughts moved on since then?

❖ What thoughts do you have now on the possibility of an afterlife? To what extent are you influenced by particular scriptures, relative to your own experience?

❖ What kind of God do you want to believe in? One that gives us all the time we need to sort out our wrongs, or one that condemns us without a second chance?

❖ Assuming there is a heavenly state, what is its purpose?

❖ What would you see as your ideal heaven?

❖ Do you believe in a God of Love, or a God of wrath and judgement?

SPIRIT: Meanings

THERE ARE MANY DIFFERENT BELIEFS about the afterlife in the Bible. In the Old Testament, a prevalent and ancient belief was in sheol, a shadowy and rather hopeless state where the dead did not praise God (e.g. Psalm 88:10). In those times, life was about living on through grand-children and reputation. Ideas of spiritual continuation began to emerge in writings such as Isaiah 26:19, 'Your dead shall rise …' With growing conster-nation over the fate of the earthly kingdom of Israel, hopes grew of a spiritual 'new Jerusalem', so that by the time of Jesus many believed in the possibility of a resurrection of the righteous dead, to become inhabitants of the glorious city of God. Into this arena Jesus introduced the new hope of entry into the kingdom of God not through righteousness but through faith and through the grace of God.

PRAYER

Father, I place my life in your hands.
In death, as in life, I know I shall depend on your forgiving grace,
for what am I but a foolish child, struggling over my lessons?
Where can I go from here, but to a new place of learning?
When I have learned all, then I will be at peace.

THE ANIMAL KINGDOM

'… no one can enter the kingdom of God without being born of water and of Spirit. What is born of the flesh is flesh, and what is born of the Spirit is spirit.' (NRSV)
— John 3:5–6. See also 1 Peter 1:23

MIND: Food for thought

THE BUTTERFLY IS A SYMBOL OF CHANGE, the change that is required of all of us before we can reach our own spiritual potential. The life cycle of the butterfly describes our own journey through different stages. The first stage is of satisfying physical needs and hungers, where we live a primarily material life. Many of us seem to stay in this stage a very long time! Next is a period of inner change, brought about by the rightness of the time and the nature of our own selves. This change requires the undoing of all that we thought we were, the dissolving of our pride, our opinions, our values, our securities and beliefs. All goes into the melting pot and although it is not lost, our past is redefined. If we can recognise the time for what it is, we need to withdraw and shelter ourselves, as though in a cocoon, for in the process we lose hold of our old identity, and with it a degree of self-confidence. Only then can the butterfly emerge, glorious creature of light and summer sun. Our journey may not happen in clearly defined stages and may fluctuate for years between the caterpillar and the chrysalis, with brief joyous moments where we feel sun on our wings and a sudden rush of insight. The rebirth may come in this earth life or it may come after the shells of our bodies have been left behind, but at some point it is the birthright of all.

BODY: What do you do?

SPIRITUAL REBIRTH, like our first birth, is not necessarily easy. The real struggle is in seeing ourselves unravelled like the elastic inside a broken golf ball. We thought we knew ourselves, then suddenly it all changes. We find that we cannot have confidence in ourselves, we cannot help ourselves, we do not understand the significance of our being as well as we thought we did. At this point we have to learn to trust not ourselves but God. It is as though we are forced into handing over control because we finally have to admit that we are nothing, when we had always hoped to be something. It is the death of our ego. Until it happens, we fight with the idea. When it happens, like the birth of a baby we cannot stop it, and in the end we realise we have received only blessing, despite the pain.

❖ When you sense change in your life does it frighten you, or thrill you?

❖ Where are you on the caterpillar-chrysalis-butterfly journey?

SPIRIT: Meanings

THE ACCOUNT from which the above quotation is taken, where Nicodemus, a Jewish leader, visits Jesus secretly, reveals the need for mystical rebirth. To know God's power working in our lives like the glory of butterfly wings, we have to be transformed. We have to make a transition from physical to spiritual. But it doesn't just come through our own effort; there is a right time that suddenly becomes apparent. We might be proud of ourselves as successful caterpillars, but this pride means nothing when the time comes to grow wings. In fact, we don't change at all until we lose our pride. As the story of Job demonstrates, not even righteousness spares us from being brought down in the eyes of the world. God does not see with the eyes of the world. In the final chapter, God reveals truth to Job, who rejoices. He finds his wings but only after developing the humility to acknowledge that it is God who has the power.

PRAYER

Lord of Life, take me and change me,
undo the old and breathe into me a new spirit of freedom and joy.

73

'Do not seek revenge or bear a grudge against one of your people, but love your neighbour as yourself … The foreigner living among you must be treated as one of your native-born. Love him as yourself.' — Leviticus 19:18 & 34 (NIV)

MIND: Food for thought

WHILE SPENDING TIME at a spiritual centre some years ago, I took part in a workshop where we were asked to look into a mirror and say 'I love you.' This simple request elicited a dramatic response: one lady present just would not, or could not, speak to herself thus; she burst into tears and left not only the workshop but the centre, saying this was not what she had come for. When Jesus, quoting from Leviticus, said we must love one another as much as we love ourselves, he meant a lot. The measure we use for others will be used for ourselves; there must be balance. I equate cats with the poise and dignity of self-love. They – on the whole – do as they please, go where they please, get what they want and enjoy the best of two worlds, domesticity and the wild. They are self-interested, but at the same time they are often affectionate companions and a great source of comfort. Jesus saw it as only natural that we would have some degree of self-respect and self-love. He did not say it was wrong to love ourselves but that we should be just as concerned about others, as our equals.

BODY: What do you do?

❖ How do you find balance between the understanding that you are entitled to love yourself, and the call to take up your cross to follow Jesus? (Matthew 10:38)

❖ What do you like, or love, most about yourself?

❖ What is the best thing you could do for yourself? Why don't you do it? Could you do the same for somebody else too?

❖ Where is true peace of mind: in financial security, in a firm and loving relationship, in knowledge of the love of God, or something else?

❖ In what situations do you put other people's material interests before or alongside your own?

❖ Consider the lives of people you consider to be genuinely selfless. Are they able to be materially selfless because they have found a higher spiritual satisfaction? If not, what compels them to act thus?

SPIRIT: Meanings

ONLY WHEN WE HAVE A HEALTHY SELF-RESPECT can we really set out to achieve what we want, not what others want from us. But what do we want? The most precious goals are surely not material, but those states of mind that keep us forever in peace and lightness of being. Our self-interest needs to be directed to spiritual goals. We must learn to be self-interested only in finding our way to God; for the rule to love God with our whole heart and soul and mind is the only commandment placed above the rule to love our neighbour as ourselves. We must seek God's love for ourselves, we must seek God's peace for ourselves, above all else. But, having found it, we must also give that love and that peace to others. Other self-interests drop away when we reach out for these true goals, and we realise that our self-love is, paradoxically, not expressed in grasping, selfish, egotistical, power-hungry, boorish behaviour, but in learning to walk close to God, which leads to naturally selfless behaviour.

PRAYER

Father, you love me and you want the best for me.
Help me to love myself enough to seek the peace and joy of your presence.
Help me to love others enough to pass on that same joyful peace.

*'When the boys grew up, Esau was a skilful hunter, a man of the field,
while Jacob was a quiet man, living in tents.'* (NRSV)

— Genesis 25:27

MIND: Food for thought

THE QUOTATION ABOVE reflects a real struggle in the history of ancient culture where hunting and gathering gave way to settled farming. Esau is the close-to-nature lover of the mountains, home of the deer and wild goats; Jacob is relatively refined, concerned with the domesticated flock: 'civilised'. Two men, different traits, or symbols of changing relationships with nature. Even in Bible times there was no expectation that all should fit the same mould. People were free to express their individual personalities, but at the same time the roles that men and women took on were much more tightly defined. In a time when birth-control was not really an option, women were very much associated with the home, children and cooking, yet they also had opportunities for managing business, and for engaging in trade (see Proverbs 31). The trouble was, the women were never free, unlike the men. They belonged either to their father or to their husband; their official status was not really much better than that of a slave. Deer too have a very patriarchal society: the males are seen as noble, virile and powerful, as perhaps epitomised by the image of Herne, ancient Lord of the Forest, who bore the great antlers of a stag. But the does are submissive, the beautiful, gentle, passive prizes of mating contests.

BODY: What do you do?

❖ We can at once admire qualities of animals and know how we are different. We can appreciate the dignity of a stag, the gentleness of a doe, but we do not have to take deer-nature completely on board for we are human, able to make choices. A man might wish to emulate a stag, but female deer are so submissive that a woman might choose a more emancipated species. Our society, with its heightened awareness of equality, is moving away from a deer-like culture, but will another animal role-model take its place?

❖ Which animals display the characteristics you most admire?

❖ Much ink is spilt on differences between the sexes. In animals we simply observe these differences and make use of them where appropriate. Is it right to do the same for ourselves or does that create unhelpful stereotypes?

❖ To what extent does your worshipping community or your social group demonstrate the love of Jesus as its primary role model? When does it fall prey to stereotype and become more like the old 'deer society'?

SPIRIT: Meanings

B ECAUSE THE BIBLE REFLECTS the time in which it was written, it inevitably contains material concerning gender roles and characteristics that we might not feel are appropriate in modern society. It reflects a time when people fell into distinct, almost pre-ordained roles. Men were in charge, women were their property. Very like deer society! Yet Jesus, despite being a man of his time, spoke to women and healed them as readily as men. He understood contemporary female concerns: wanting to have babies blessed, anxiety over catering arrangements for guests, the loss of a dowry coin, the desperate need of a widow whose son had died, a child's sickness. He didn't try to change society, he addressed individuals. He did not pass judgement but responded to need. What animal has such magnanimous and generous-hearted characteristics? In Jesus we find a real man, an ideal role model, but one as accessible to women as to men; to all types of women and all types of men. In Jesus we can set aside our perceptions of difference and concentrate on being who we are, for that is how Jesus accepts us.

PRAYER

Father, in our humanity, let us transcend those characteristics that limit and divide.
Let us explore what it is to be human, to be autonomous,
to be credited with intelligence and free will.
Let us build our communities and our society
around the sense of love Jesus showed to all.

'Is there anyone among you who, if your child asks for bread, will give a stone?
Or if the child asks for a fish, will give a snake? If you then, who are evil,
know to give good gifts to your children how much more will your father in heaven
give good things to those who ask him!' — Matthew 7:9–11 (NRSV)

MIND: Food for thought

DOGS HAVE FOUND THEIR WAY into our affections to the extent that many breeds have arisen out of the desire to have a creature to pamper, train, play with and love, almost like a perpetual child. We see them as faithful and devoted companions, loving towards the owner, yet capable of hostility towards those who appear to trespass. The Bible literature as a whole (for once there is agreement between books!) does not see dogs with this affection, but more as scavengers closely linked to hyenas or wolves than as beloved pets and trusted workers. Expressions in both the Bible and our own history are testimony to the dog's poor public image in the past: a creature subject to the blows of a master, a victim, a dirty, disreputable scavenger. Yet dogs are as we made them. It is our interference over the centuries with the interbreeding process that has produced such a variety of creatures with so many functions and peculiarities. We are responsible – we bred characteristics and we need to provide the care. The same is true for our children. We bring them into existence and we shape them according to our own perceptions of the world; it is our job to nurture them in a way that brings out their goodness, not their nastiness. All criminals are the child of some parent, and a product of the society in which they live. We may condemn an individual, but we should also look beyond them to see what kind of manure was fertilising their growth.

BODY: What do you do?

The saying 'Give a dog a bad name and hang him' springs to mind. It is easy to look for someone to blame and condemn. It is easy to find a subordinate, whether child, animal, or in some cases spouse, and vent our negative emotions on them. They are expected to take it. In no position to answer back, they simply become cowering vessels to receive our poison. This is the picture when relationships go wrong, when adults abuse their power.

❖ Where do you diffuse your negative emotions?

❖ You might know a person who seems to cower like a dog. Do you know why they seem like this? Can anything you do or say help to heal them?

❖ What difference can it make to try to understand why a person acts the way they do?

❖ At what point must someone stop blaming their upbringing and take full responsibility for their own moral decisions? When a person cannot escape early influences, can they be expected to think independently?

SPIRIT: Meanings

DOGS AND CHILDREN are brought together in the account of a foreign woman's plea to Jesus to heal her daughter. Jesus at first seems to insult the woman, yet she retorts with spirit, as though expecting banter, and gets what she wants. Pups eat up crumbs, children should be healed. In the end it did not matter that a foreign child was receiving God's grace. Divine love is for everyone. Jesus could not stop showing compassion, regardless of public opinion. Little children are not pawns in political or religious games of adults, they are innocent. The trouble is that innocent children all too often grow up in a climate of hatred, fear and ignorance, and adopt a terrible life-philosophy; they see a dog-eat-dog world and perpetuate it. Yet how can we expect them to learn gentleness and compassion, if their parents or their community know little of such things themselves? Where is the root of the blame? Against whom should we direct our anger? Jesus vented his against the hypocrisy of the religious establishment. In our culture, who should accept responsibility?

PRAYER

Father God, let the world open itself to your love, not close up in fear.
Let every parent have enough love to pass on to their children;
let the children remember that love and seek to make it grow.
Let us fill the hearts of our children with goodness and peace,
because of the future; because of their future.

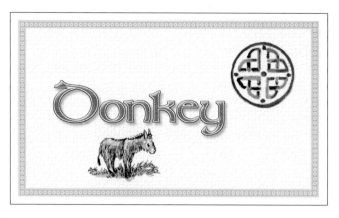

'What have I done to you that you have struck me these three times? …
Am I not your donkey, which you have ridden all your life to this day?' (NRSV)
— Numbers 22:28. See also Zechariah 9:9–10

MIND: Food for thought

DONKEYS, or asses, feature prominently in the Bible. They have always been beasts of burden, gentle, unassuming and strong. Sanctified by their association with Jesus as a baby in arms and later as he entered Jerusalem in fulfilment of Zechariah's prophecy, they even bear a cross on their backs. But of all creatures mentioned in the Bible, it is the donkey alone that has been given a voice. In Numbers 22 we read of Balaam, summoned by the King of Moab to curse the people of Israel. Although reluctant at first, knowing it was against God's wishes, he agreed to go in the end, but found his donkey uncooperative. Balaam could not see an angel barring the way, but the donkey could and refused to move, hence the beating. God opened the donkey's mouth to let it object. This faithful creature did not deserve to be beaten and God gave it the right to say so. Faithful service is to be acknowledged, and as servants of society we have the right to speak if we are abused, or if we see abuse. Only one chose to keep silence: 'He was oppressed and he was afflicted, yet he did not open his mouth; like a lamb that is led to the slaughter … so he did not open his mouth.' (Isaiah 53:7) The Suffering Servant, seen by Christians as Christ himself, withheld his right to object because he knew there was a higher purpose in his death.

BODY: What do you do?

THE ASSOCIATION with diligent service might lead us to think about our own occupations. Are you ever like Balaam, mistreating those who serve you instead of loving them?

❖ Are you exploited and abused? You must pray for help, for God to give you a strong voice to defend yourself, rather than heaping up resentment. Are you worth less than a donkey?

❖ Is your workplace a place that reflects the words of Paul in Galatians 3:28? 'There is neither … slave nor free, male nor female, for you are all one in Christ Jesus.' Can you hold on to your spiritual integrity at work? We would do well to learn from those faiths that intersperse the day with prayer or contemplation, and that encourage constant mindfulness of God's presence. If we do not work 'to the glory of God' then our work is ultimately useless.

SPIRIT: Meanings

THE DONKEY in the Palm Sunday story really did take God to work that day, and for ever onward was blessed. The donkey that carried Balaam also met with God's angel, and was vindicated. Do we ever manage to carry Christ in our humble efforts, or might it be better to let Christ carry us? For while the donkey is known as a beast of burden, so too did Jesus promise, 'Come to me all who labour and are heavy laden and I will give you rest, for my yoke is light and my burden is easy.' We were not meant to be slaves, after all, but 'one in Christ Jesus' (Galatians 3:28). We have the right to our dignity, and we are offered freedom in Christ that can transform service into joy. We are all beloved of God and it is God's will that we walk in the Light, not under a shadow of oppression or ridicule. It does not help the cause for Christians to be seen as 'nice', timid and subservient – this looks too much like weakness. Remember, 'God did not give us a spirit of cowardice, but rather a spirit of power and of love and of self-discipline.' (2 Timothy 1:7)

PRAYER

Christ who carries our burdens still,
Christ who led with humility,
Christ, King of peace and true nobility,
let me serve joyfully, according to your will.

81

'Then he took the seven loaves and the fish, and when he had given thanks, he broke them and gave them to the disciples, and they in turn to the people.' (NIV)
— Matthew 15:36

MIND: Food for thought

THE WORD FISH was used as an acronym by early Christian communities, a codified statement of faith in times of persecution. The letters of the Greek word for fish, I-ch-th-u-s stand for Iesous (Jesus), Christos, Theou (of God), huios, (son), soterios (Saviour), or perhaps the verb 'he saves'. That is, Jesus Christ, Son of God, Saviour, or Jesus Christ, Son of God, saves. The concept of sonship has roots in the Old Testament. In Exodus 4:22 for example Israel is described as God's firstborn; the Israelites were entitled to call themselves children of God. Psalm 2 is the origin of the words 'You are my son, today I have begotten you', as part of a promise concerning a king. The paternal relationship was formalised through the institution of the Davidic covenant: God declared to King David that he would be a father to Solomon and Solomon would be his son. The term was thus not without precedent and was used by New Testament writers to emphasise the close bond between Jesus and God, but also Jesus and the nation's history of kingship, covenant and longing for a messiah. The Celts too were interested in the symbolism of the fish. Tales were told of Fintan, a Salmon of Knowledge. The one who caught this fish and ate it would be blessed with unsurpassed wisdom; it was therefore sought after by many, yet stumbled upon fortuitously by those who were meant to find it.

BODY: What do you do?

❖ How do you see Jesus's relationship with God? Look at all the titles ascribed to him by writers in the New Testament: Son of God, Son of Man, Messiah, Christ, Lamb of God, Teacher, Master, Lord, Shepherd and so on. Each of these titles is worth tracing in both the Old and New Testaments, and studying. Which title do you feel best reflects your understanding of Jesus? In studying the titles, are you prepared for your current image of Jesus to change?

❖ What does the ritual of drinking wine and eating broken bread mean to you? This too is a subject worthy of both study and contemplation.

SPIRIT: Meanings

I USED TO THINK that there was something slightly ridiculous in using a fish to remind myself of Christ, but the more I contemplated the sealskin, the more appropriate it seemed. Fish live in water and water can represent the infinity of God. Fish breathe, sleep, eat and have their being in water, just as we do in air. Jesus was closer to God than we are; he belonged with God and was one with God. The fact that seals eat fish seems to spoil the analogy at first glance, but then what is the symbol of the eucharist if not the consuming of Christ's body and blood? The quotation above, from the feeding of the four thousand, reflects or anticipates the imagery of the last supper: the fishes' bodies were broken like the bread, and like Christ's body. We can return to the myth of the Salmon of Knowledge for, like the one who ate Fintan, any who bring Christ within themselves gain wisdom and insight beyond the eyes of the world.

PRAYER

Christ, be part of me,
nourish me, bless me with your wisdom.
Christ within me, live through me,
lead me always on to greater depths.

'Then the temple police went back to the chief priests and Pharisees,
who asked them, "Why did you not arrest him?" The police answered,
"Never has anyone spoken like this!"' — John 7:45 (NRSV)

MIND: Food for thought

THE FOX IN BRITAIN occupies a uniquely contentious place. It is at once hunter and quarry, wild yet at home in the urban world, loved and protected by some, hated by others. Fox hunting is an issue on which most people have an opinion one way or the other; and this debate in itself has been seen as a dividing point between town and country dwellers, the implication being that neither really understands the other. But the foxes of course are blissfully unaware of all the controversy – they just get on with their lives. But in the process they come a little too close to disrupting the human status quo and are not welcomed for it. We don't like people who rock the boat, who 'put a cat among the pigeons'; we like to think that we are in control. But the way we respond to this animal as it goes about its business says more about ourselves than it does about the fox. The context of the quotation above is that Jesus had gone 'under cover' to a major Jewish festival, and there suddenly appeared, causing admiration in some and hostility in others. His aborted arrest was discussed, and Nicodemus, one of the leaders, spoke in Jesus's defence, arguing that he had the right to a fair hearing before he was condemned. Nicodemus speaks even now on the side of fairness and justice, against those who are quick to cry for blood.

BODY: What do you do?

❖ What is your opinion on fox hunting? What is at the heart of your argument: pity for the fox, pity for hens, local economy, or something else?

❖ Who might a fox personify? What might the act of hunting for sport represent?

❖ Whether the fox is a perpetrator of violence against domestic animals or not, can avoidable cruelty be justified? Is cruelty against animals ever justified? Do you eat meat? What do you know about and think about battery farming? Do you or a loved one ever need medication? What do you know about and think about experiments on animals?

❖ If a person has perpetrated acts of violence, does the voice of Nicodemus become irrelevant?

❖ When did you last write a letter to defend an innocent prisoner of conscience or supported them in some other way?

SPIRIT: Meanings

THE PRIME EXAMPLE of someone who disrupted the status quo and was removed because of the embarrassment he was causing the establishment was Jesus. And the authorities didn't stop at removal; they did their utmost to make sure he wouldn't come back. Unfortunately for them, he surpassed their imaginations and as a consequence his message was spread more powerfully than ever before. While such acts can produce martyrs, in Jesus's case the authorities didn't create a martyr, they set free the Christ. Some 'foxes' have a message of disruption that needs to be heard; we need to listen carefully to the message we receive, for fear of missing truth. Yet the converse is also true: we need to be on the look out for mischief. For there is a voice of fear and hatred that is spoken sometimes by the seditious and sometimes by those who hunt down the sedition. Recalling the quotation above, we have to ask ourselves if we can speak like Nicodemus, whether we sympathise with the 'fox' or not.

PRAYER

Father, when I feel tempted to go hunting adversaries,
keep my response within the boundaries of your will;
keep my mind centred on you, my heart open to you,
that I may meet turmoil with wisdom.

'My heart exults in the Lord;
my strength is exalted in my God.' (NRSV)
— 1 Samuel 2:1

MIND: Food for thought

THE BEAT OF THE HEART symbolises the innate life in us that we share with every creature. This is the symbol of the wild part of us, the spiral of wisdom through knowing our instincts and being close to the earth. This is the part of us that would rather take off back into the woods or the mountains and oceans to lose ourselves and find ourselves. This is the symbol that reassures us that it is acceptable to sit out all night gazing at the moon, or to wade through a stream just to climb a tree, or to lie with our face in the grass so we can see the insects. It is acceptable to explore our fascination with the world around us just as children do, for in so doing we gain confidence, and we start to remember what it is to be alive. We re-learn to walk with quiet, strong steps, in rhythm with life. We re-learn to listen and watch so that we know what is behind and on all sides. We begin to notice trees and creatures as individuals and to respond when we see change in them as though they were friends. We begin to feel at home outside and safe out in the dark; we begin to sense the hidden world of Spirit around us, for the heartbeat of the earth is always there.

BODY: What do you do?

THROUGH WATCHING AND FEELING the natural world around us, it becomes possible sometimes to sense something Other, a great power, the surging, vital energy of creation. Trees and plants are not inanimate objects; they are living entities with a definite sense of presence, an energy that almost cries out to be noticed. All matter is condensed energy and all matter that breathes has a miraculous quality of its own. The whole natural world is buzzing and teeming with the spirit of life, Ruah, the Hebrew concept of the breath of God. Having become aware of the energy we come to realise how much we need it and how much we should be part of it. The symbol of the heartbeat calls us to rediscover the divine in nature, for we need to be filled with the same exuberance and strength. This is not 'nature worship'; it is realising the presence of spirit in all life, and rejoicing in the creative energy we find all around us.

SPIRIT: Meanings

THE HEARTBEAT REMINDS US that we are animal and need to make peace with all with which we share this world. The drumming and dancing is beginning again among those who have moved back to the edges of the woods, and the rhythm is almost irresistible. It drums out the heartbeat of the earth, of all the creatures, of the trees, and if we too can but slip out into the woods and hills, the drums will beat in resonance with our own heartbeats. When all bring themselves back to the dance, then the spirit will be there at the heart of the drum, singing for joy, the true Lord of the Dance. The spirit is not just about people, it is about life; not just about oneness of humans, but oneness of all. Love does not stop with people; every sparrow is precious for it too contains that spark. All belong together in a great and beautiful dance, a drum-dance through the cycles of life, death and new life; a dance of celebration and harmony.

PRAYER

Mother God, whose heartbeat was everything to me in my infancy,
whose heartbeat defined the rhythm of my very existence in your spirit-womb,
remind me of the unfaltering beat, the endless dance.
Lead me back to the circle to take my place.
Let my heart beat as one with you, and with your living world.

'Keep me as the apple of your eye,
hide me in the shadow of your wings …' (NIV)
— Psalm 17:8. See also: Matthew 23:37, Luke 13:34

MIND: Food for thought

A MOTHER BIRD WAS CHOSEN both by the writer of Psalm 17 and by Jesus to represent the mother-like nature of God. Hens gather up their chicks so that they can hardly be seen under the mass of downy feathers.; so warm and safe, surrounded by softness. In Matthew 23 and Luke 13, Jesus is quoted as saying he longed to gather the people of Jerusalem together under his care, 'as a hen gathers a chick under her wings', but they were not willing; they resisted. Jesus mourned that, instead, they were a harsh people who killed messengers of God. There is a connection between these quotations and Jesus's statements elsewhere about children. In Matthew 11:25 for example Jesus laments over the impending downfall of great and proud towns in Israel, but in the same verse praises God that marvels were revealed not to the 'wise and learned', but to little children. Elsewhere we read of Jesus's willingness to bless the children his disciples intended to send away, and his statement that to enter the kingdom of heaven we must be like a child (Matthew 18:3). Jesus connected acceptance of his message with a certain capacity to be childlike. In the context of the hen, perhaps, it is the willingness to be completely enveloped by God's love.

BODY: What do you do?

❖ Behind the adult exterior, there is a child in everyone. While in everyday life we need to interact on an adult level, we also need to be in touch with the feelings that come from our child.

❖ Do you listen to your child-voice and try to understand how it affects you?

❖ Do you feel at peace with your childhood, or were there times when you felt unloved? Does that affect your ability to love and live now?

❖ Are you able to offer tenderness and comfort when you see a need?

❖ How do you show respect for the feelings and views of children you encounter?

❖ What quality do you think Jesus saw in children that he meant us to emulate?

SPIRIT: Meanings

I N RECALLING THE QUOTATION above from Psalm 17, we put ourselves in the place of those hard-hearted city-dwellers who rejected the love of Jesus. We can go like a tiny chick to the delicious warmth and safety of our God, who is as much like a mother as a father to us. We are not asked to be fearless and clever, we are not expected always to take the lead or prove our own prowess; that doesn't matter. What matters is that we know where to take refuge when we need to. It is safe to feel like a child with God; in fact, there is some quality common to children that we need to rediscover, perhaps the trust, perhaps the innocence or spontaneity, perhaps the smallness. When we have found that quality, then somehow we are closer to the feather-filled kingdom of Heaven.

PRAYER

Gentle Mother God,
nestle me in the bliss of your softness,
hold me, in my smallness, close to your heart.
Whisper words of love
and let me be at peace, safe in my vulnerability,
safe to show my childlike love for you.
Gentle Mother God,
hide me under the shadow of your wings.

'Your kingdom come, your will be done
on earth as it is in heaven.' (NIV)
— Matthew 6:10

MIND: Food for thought

BEES, LIKE ANTS, have received much praise in Western culture for the industrious and cooperative manner in which they live. Napoleon for example took the bee as his symbol for the great working classes. Before that, ironically, they featured in the heraldry of nobility, as a symbol of industry and loyalty to the sovereign, while Pliny the Elder, writing in the first century AD, remarked on their single-minded devotion to the common good. Bee colonies however, while fascinating, may not present the idyll we would wish for. The queens can never rear their own young, the workers can never produce them, and most of the drones are superfluous and killed off in the autumn. Bee society, while highly successful in perpetuating the existence of bees, requires that individuals are expendable and follow a clearly defined role that is their whole *raison d'être*. The Bible documents the thoughts of a people who formed a society based on their understanding of the word of God. It was intended to be an idyll, a holy nation, a model of social justice; yet instead of peace, there was conflict. Unlike bees, people have the right to exercise independent thought, a fact that produces saints, tyrants and those in between. Many have produced theories on the perfect society. Each in turn proves inadequate, but why? Perhaps we should return to Pliny, who saw the importance of working for the common good. But what is the common good? What is the global good? Will we ever agree?

BODY: What do you do?

* How would your own utopia, your ideal society, function? On what principles would it be based?

* What are the consequences, do you think, of a government imposing values, motives and directives on professional bodies such as teachers and doctors? Where is the balance between public accountability and respect for trained experts?

* Who in society might feel undervalued, abandoned and superfluous and why? Have you ever felt this way?

* Do you feel that you exist entirely to be of service to society, or do you have the right to 'time out'? Do you live to work, or work to live?

* Have you ever traced references to the kingdom of God or the kingdom of heaven in the gospels? What did Jesus mean when he used this term? Where is this kingdom?

SPIRIT: Meanings

JESUS LIVED in a politically volatile place and time. Only a generation after his death, the very heart of the Jewish temple cult was torn down, with terrible loss of life. Jesus knew the prophecies and the nationalistic hopes for a messiah king to establish a new earthly kingdom; there is even evidence to suggest that followers wished to make Jesus a political and military leader. Yet Jesus repeatedly walked away from such a role, as demonstrated by the account of his temptation by Satan. Jesus went about his business of ministering to individuals, bringing them closer to an understanding of the spiritual kingdom, in spite of the society of his time, which largely rejected him. He did not seek to overthrow the leaders, but to lighten the hearts of the people. He did this knowing that every individual counted and was important. What can we do but let him carry on his work in our own hearts? Gradually, we hope, the consequences will spread outwards to build a network of light.

PRAYER

Lord Jesus, you died for a troubled world,
a society that could not heal itself or even love its own members.
Teach me to determine the will of the Father, that I may learn your work
of healing, of comforting, of welcoming all into your kingdom of love,
even here on Earth.

'In the night I saw a man riding on a red horse! He was standing among the myrtle trees
in the glen; and behind him were red, sorrel and white horses …
Then they spoke to the angel of the Lord … "We have patrolled the earth,
and lo, the whole earth remains at peace."' — Zechariah 1:8,11 (NRSV)

MIND: Food for thought

THE INCREDIBLE VITALITY of cave paintings and sculptures bears witness to the awe and sense of worth attached to wild animals such as horses or ponies since people first populated the world. There is evidence for the existence of both horses and the smaller breeds of ponies in the British Isles since long before the Roman invasion of AD43. The indigenous wild breeds are particularly renowned for their intelligence and hardiness; the larger horses were much admired by the conquering Romans who shared a mutual interest with the Celts in the horse cult of Epona. We shall never know what was in the minds of the artists who communicated their images of horses and other wild animals, or the devotees of the goddess; we can only meditate on what they might mean to us today. The quotation above is unusual in the Bible, as it connects horses with peace, unlike most texts which see the horse primarily in connection with battle. The vision is one of hope, because the king Darius has managed to bring a time of peace throughout the land. The horses appear as witnesses, almost guardians of this peace, bringers of good news. Later in Zechariah, we read that the true King of Israel would come not on a war horse but on a humble donkey, 'and he shall command peace to the nations'. The time of the war horse would be over; its role instead, as in the vision, would be to monitor the peace.

BODY: What do you do?

YOU MIGHT ENJOY using the vision of Zechariah in meditation. Imagine yourself as the rider, at one with your horse as you set out on a journey to find peace. The Bible uses myrtle; to us the poppy might have a similar significance. So ride together, sensing the muscle beneath you, the rhythm of breathing and hoof beat, the shared understanding of urgency and pleasure in the freedom of the gallop; ride towards fields where you know there was once warfare, where you know there were terrible deaths and great fear. You may sense the terror still there in the air, yet you have come to lay it to rest, the ghosts of battle must find peace. Ride on until you come to the open fields. All around, as you pass, poppies unfurl. A sea of red surrounds you as you gallop on, but not a sea of blood, a sea of delicate flower petals. You know the memories of these fields; but you see also a new hope; beauty where there was once misery, peace where there was once war. Keep that image with you and strive always to be an emissary of peace.

SPIRIT: Meanings

THE SHIFT from an association between horses and war to a new, peaceful role can be linked conceptually with the well-loved quotation from Isaiah 2:4. 'They shall beat their swords into ploughshares, and their spears into pruning hooks; nation shall not lift up sword against nation, neither shall they learn war any more.' Given the biblical preoccupation with war horses, Isaiah might have added 'They shall train their horses as swift envoys of peace between the nations, neither shall they learn to break skulls with their hooves any more.' Again in Isaiah we can find reference to myrtle trees, linked in Zechariah's vision to the horses, and again there is the image of transition from desolation to joy and peace. '... Instead of the thorn shall come up the cypress, instead of the brier shall come up the myrtle' (Isaiah 55:12–13). We are thus presented with a vision of hope, a vision we must all work towards realising, one in which the horse, standing amongst the myrtle bushes, plays a symbolic role. Let the horse or the pony become a symbol of change, of laying down arms, of seeking peace with one another and with the natural world.

PRAYER

Father, inspire us to ride with the horses of peace, through fields that once screamed with war, but may yet be strewn with flowers. Let us never lose hope of the vision, let us never cease from seeking peace for this world.

'Master, you handed over to me five talents;
see, I have made five more talents.' (NRSV)
— Matthew 25:20

MIND: Food for thought

MAGPIES HAVE A REPUTATION for collecting shiny objects; their alleged habit makes an apt focus for meditation on the accumulation of wealth. The prevalent belief in the Old Testament was that wealth indicated God's favour, because it was not possible to prosper without God's blessing. The rich, in turn, could demonstrate their righteousness by helping the deserving poor, financing public buildings and sitting as impartial judges in local affairs. This was why it was such a shock to Job that he suddenly became sick and destitute. His friends were convinced that he must secretly have sinned, yet he was adamant that he was righteous before God. Hence also the astonishment of the disciples in Matthew 19:25, when told it was easier for a camel to get through the eye of a needle than for a rich person to enter the kingdom of God. Jesus's call to poverty was a barrier to the rich young ruler: he came to Jesus confident in his own righteousness and went away discovering he would never come to God through his own efforts. Rather than being an asset, his wealth was a hindrance and an encumbrance that he was not prepared to let go of. The true treasure is the presence of God, but this is easier to grasp if our hands are otherwise empty.

BODY: What do you do?

JESUS IS RECORDED as saying, in the context of warning us not to hoard material wealth, 'Where your treasure is, there your heart will be also.' (Matthew 6:21) Where does your heart lie?

❖ What item are you most attached to? Why? Is it something that brings you closer to God through sharing, perhaps like a musical instrument, or is it something that makes you feel separate from God and even from other people?

❖ What talents do you have? Which of these have you ever used for the benefit of others, or in exploration of spiritual depth?

❖ Since giving up all we own reduces us to dependence on the state, and is thus a drain on resources better used in supporting the elderly and infirm, what feasible interpretation or alternative can you think of to the first-century suggestion to give all to the poor and follow Jesus? Is entry into holy orders the only option?

SPIRIT: Meanings

THE QUOTATION ABOVE is taken from a parable of a master who left his wealth with servants. Two managed to increase his wealth, one did nothing with it. We are entrusted with different levels of wealth, but this wealth has potential, it has energy. Money is neither inherently good nor evil, it depends what we use it for. But our wealth does not stop at money; the parable has an accidental pun in English, for we can also take the word 'talent' literally, rather than meaning a Palestinian coin. We have creative gifts and abilities that we can develop, and again it is what we do with these skills that is important. If we become so self-absorbed that our attention is channelled only into self, then our activity bars us from God. If our energy is put towards exploring the spiritual dimension, then we are drawn closer. Jesus wanted the rich young ruler to use his wealth to help others, and thus draw himself closer to God. But it may not always be money that stands in the way; there may be some 'hidden talent' that needs to be offered up, in order for us to receive true blessing.

PRAYER

Father, let me be generous with what I have.
Let me use my gifts creatively, for the benefit of others, not just myself.
Let nothing stand between me and you, for you are the greatest treasure of all.

Mole

'... and if you call out for insight and cry aloud for understanding, and if you look for it as for silver and search for it as for hidden treasure, then you will understand the fear of the Lord and find the knowledge of God.' — Proverbs 2:3–5 (NIV)

MIND: Food for thought

I HAD A PARTICULAR FASCINATION for moles as a child. I read books about them, drew them, collected mole toys, wrote stories, watched molehills, and longed to see one. I was captivated by the idea of knowing they were very close, yet also out of reach. It was as though they lived in a different world altogether. I did see one eventually, but not while I was searching. Moles are rather an enigma to most people as they are so rarely seen yet leave evidence of their presence everywhere. While most small furry creatures are naturally shy and elusive, the mole has gone one step further and simply bypasses the owl hunting grounds. It has found another world to exploit and has little need to leave this haven where its needs are effectively met. Here, it can feel relatively safe, master of its own environment. To me, the mole represents the object of our searching, that which we want more than anything. We can study, use our creativity, watch and wait like faithful servants but what we seek comes when we aren't expecting it, out of the blue – in God's time, not ours.

BODY: What do you do?

❖ What is it that you are searching for with your whole heart? How do you go about it?

❖ In your search for wisdom, where do you look? Books? Nature? In places of worship? You may assimilate a great deal of opinion, dogma, rhetoric and incomplete knowledge before you hit on real wisdom, but how do you recognise it when you find it? It has to strike a chord in your heart. It rings true, it connects with something you already knew, that finally you can try to articulate.

❖ How do you respond to the words of Jesus: 'Ask and you will receive, seek and you will find, knock and the door shall be opened to you?' What should you be asking for? On which door do you knock? (Matthew 7:7)

SPIRIT: Meanings

WHAT IS IT WE REALLY SEARCH FOR? The seal searches the depths of the oceans, the mole searches the tunnels of the earth and we search the depths of our minds for hidden wisdom, for God. But despite the importance of study, which can give us a sense of discernment and help us to recognise that which we seek, and despite the importance of demonstrating diligence and determination in our tirelessness, we don't find God in study or in waiting for a vision. God will catch us napping, God appears and it is for us to notice and appreciate. How often does the Presence draw near, yet we are asleep? The truth is that, like moles, the wisdom we seek is there all the time under the surface. Perhaps simply knowing it is there is enough to enthuse us, or are we too like Thomas who was not satisfied until he had seen with his own eyes?

PRAYER

Lord, you said that if we seek we will find and if we ask we will receive.
What is worth seeking but wisdom?
What is worth requesting, but that we find the Spirit of Truth, there at our hearts?
Lead us to discover our own spiritual depth.

'Let the little children come to me and do not stop them; for it is to such as these that the kingdom of heaven belongs.' (NRSV)
— Matthew 19:14

MIND: Food for thought

THE OTTER HAS MANY ATTRIBUTES, including the capacity it shares with some other mammals to continue playing, even into adulthood. It is at once a lithe and highly adapted hunter, and a creature that can take obvious delight in its environment. While there is much theory on the 'play' behaviours of humans and other animals, it is safe to say that they include preparation for adulthood, establishing pecking orders, developing bonds, training the body, and relaxing and stimulating the mind. Educationalists acknowledge that we learn best when we are enjoying ourselves, particularly when we are actively involved. We should never stop learning, so we should never stop playing; we all know the old adage, 'All work and no play makes Jack a dull boy.' Jesus seems to have shared this attitude; he was certainly not averse to merry-making, to the point where he was accused of being a glutton and a drunkard (Matthew 11:19). Yet, as Jesus went on to say, he would be vindicated by the outcome of his ministry; it would become apparent to all that his willingness to relax and be merry, even with undesirables, was founded in wisdom. Not only was Jesus enjoying himself, he was providing the ministry that those people needed. It was a way of deepening their relationship with him and thus with God.

BODY: What do you do?

❖ Do you normally enjoy your work? If not, why not? Can you do anything to make your work more rewarding? Can you change? Do you need to look for a new occupation, which has more intrinsic meaning for you?

❖ We sometimes encounter managers who employ intimidation, even fear, to increase productivity. Is fear ever a greater motivator than love? How do you think you should respond to such an employer?

❖ How do you relax? What do you do with your leisure time? Do you waste it, or do you use it constructively?

SPIRIT: Meanings

JESUS COULD NEVER BE ACCUSED of being po-faced, but he also never wasted any time. There was a sense of urgency pushing his ministry on, he was intent on bringing the news of the kingdom to the people. He demonstrated that sometimes the best way of teaching the love of God was just to be with people, relax with them, share jokes and stories and enjoy a good party. That he emerged from these social encounters with integrity intact demonstrates his own strength of mind. He was purposeful in his 'play'; there was reason to it, it was constructive. He could enjoy it without being swallowed up by the meaninglessness and corruption that might have troubled his companions; in fact he showed them an alternative way of seeing things. We too are at liberty to seek enjoyment in what we do – in fact the more pleasure we get out of our work, the more productive we are.

PRAYER

Lord Jesus,
You knew how to have a good time, you knew how to relax but also how to enjoy
your work. Help me to love what I do; help me to bring that love to others as I work
and as I play. In all things, let the love grow.

'Can a blind person guide a blind person?
Will not both fall into a pit?' (NRSV)
— Luke 6:39

MIND: Food for thought

THE OWL, perfectly adapted to take advantage of the night, becomes an eloquent symbol of our own capacity to come to terms with the darkness, the unknown, the great unspoken dread that there is a huge universe out there and we are horribly alone. Why else do we shut ourselves away at night behind curtains, with as many lights on as possible? If we think too hard we start to remember that the stars are not pretty little dots of light but massive balls of burning gas so far away that we have no hope of reaching them. If the nearest stars are so far away, then how far away must God be? We live in the daylight because it hurts our heads to think such big, frightening thoughts. In this modern world of scientific understanding, we cannot even imagine that God sits above the sphere pulling strings. We know too much. The dark is a time for lighting fires, finding friends, singing and telling stories. It is a time when we allow companionship to bring us through.

PRAYER

God of inner light, God of inner sight,
reveal yourself to me in a way I can understand,
give me yourself in a way I can accept,
Bless me with the support of prayerful fellowship;
that I may not feel lonely and afraid even when I am alone.

BODY: What do you do?

❧ How do you feel about the dark? What experiences can you recall where you had strong feelings of fear, excitement, happiness or unhappiness?

❧ Do you ever experience feelings of doubt, that there is no God, that you are all alone?

❧ How do you believe in God? Have you 'created' an emotional prop, a kind of Big Daddy that is always on your side, or do you have genuine experiences that speak personally to you? Have you reasoned your God into existence because you cannot bear the possibility that otherwise you are alone? Or have you really sensed something other? Have you reasoned your God out of existence? Do these questions make you feel uncomfortable? If not, what makes you so self-assured in your own personal beliefs?

❧ What situations are your 'night's, when you feel most alone? How do you approach others who appear to be in the dark themselves? Are you a blind person trying to lead the blind? Are you a light shining in the darkness? How dependent are you on others to see you through?

SPIRIT: Meanings

TO SOME, night-time is the only reality. There may as well be no sun for they never see it. Yet without the sun there would be no life, so even night dwellers are dependent on the light. Some people allow no possibility for the fact that there might be a God, perhaps because they see no place for God to reside – the universe stretches on with no heavenly cloud detected as yet. The sheer meaninglessness of life in such a state must be hard to take. Living a Godless life, knowing the vastness of space and the smallness of ourselves, must be a very lonely position to be in. But surely there is hope, for the sheer presence of life is evidence of sunlight, and if there is life then there is movement and growth; and if there is growth then we can grow in wisdom, we can look for value and meaning. To see this way requires not outward eyes but an inner eye. We wait not for lamps to light the night but for an inner lamp to illuminate our inner life, so that whatever is going on outside, we are not afraid because inside we know the sun is always there, somewhere. It is easier to find this light in the company of others; we are drawn to those who can support us, where we can feel a sense of warmth and security. It takes huge strength to face the dark alone.

'What God has made clean you must not call profane.' (NRSV)
— Acts 10:15

MIND: Food for thought

THERE WERE MANY LAWS on cleanliness in the culture of Jesus's day; Mosaic law gave instructions concerning every aspect of life, and the circumstances in which an item, animal or human might be declared untouchable or unclean. (The reasons behind these laws are much debated by historians, anthropologists and theologians, an area worth delving into.) Swine were not to be eaten, along with many other animals. One could become polluted by contact with a corpse, a leper, a woman at certain times of the month, and so on. Significantly, during his ministry Jesus came into physical contact with all of these. By touching a leper, he put himself into a state of ritual impurity, but he seemed not to care. He also seemed not to care about his reputation: he frequently spoke with women in public and in their own homes, and had women providing for his needs among his followers; yet association with women was very much frowned upon in religious circles. If this was not shocking enough, he frequented the places of corrupt tax collectors and prostitutes; yet instead of contracting ritual defilement himself through his controversial behaviour, he brought healing, and gave the right to be called whole. This meant nothing less than acceptance back into society. Jesus demonstrated the acceptability of all.

BODY: What do you do?

WE ALL HAVE THINGS that fill us with revulsion, yet sometimes we either have to look beyond to the reality of a fellow creature in need, or we risk badly letting someone down. Whether it is a child, an elderly person or a drunk, sometimes we encounter individuals who have a rather unpleasant problem that we can choose to deal with or ignore.

❖ Who have you ignored in their need, because the problem seemed distasteful to you?

❖ What is it about yourself that you believe must be unacceptable to God? Has it become a barrier between you and God? What can you do to remove this barrier?

SPIRIT: Meanings

JESUS WAS NOT AFRAID to defy the religious hypocrisy of his day. Had he told the story of the Good Samaritan to children, he might have used animal characters, in which case the Samaritan would have been a pig. The children would have been conditioned to find pigs dirty, and would have been quite shocked (and probably delighted too!) that a pig could be the hero of a story. Yet Jesus knew it made no difference who a person believed themselves to be, or how society classified them; to God they were – and are – important, therefore they ought to be important to us too. It is one thing, though, to look magnanimously at others, and another to look at ourselves. It is easy to make lists of our own faults, our own reasons for being rejected by God; we do not need to deny these traits but to accept that we are still accepted despite them. We do not need to cast ourselves as pigs, or rather it is meaningless to do so, for pigs are ultimately as acceptable to God as anything else.

PRAYER

Dear God, I abase myself, knowing my own nature; I hide in shame.
But can a baby hide itself from its mother? Does it want to?
Is it possible that a part of me disgusts you so much you will not touch me?
Be my Mother God, love all of me, take away my self-reproach.

'... and they cried out in fear. But immediately Jesus spoke to them and said, "Take heart, it is I; do not be afraid."' (NRSV)
— Matthew 14: 26–36

MIND: Food for thought

WILD RABBITS SURVIVE by being ever vigilant for danger and ever ready to bolt into their tunnels for safety. On the whole, they are experts in the art of running away; the epitome of timidity and nervousness. Although rabbits are widespread these days, only the Celts of the continent would have been familiar with them; the British Isles knew only the hare until the twelfth century. While it is uncertain whether noblemen bothered to hunt for such small quarry, given the alternatives of deer and boar, they were certainly prey to larger animals and to the poor. Rabbits and hares represent the instinct for self-preservation and the emotion of fear. The hare even screams when caught. They represent the wisdom of knowing when to seek shelter, but also remind us of the extremes. We can develop an exaggerated sense of the risk we perceive, so that we feel under constant stress, and we can refuse to see danger when it threatens, thus putting ourselves and others at risk. The quotation above is an instance where Jesus's disciples experienced extreme fear but had nowhere to hide, for they were in a boat. They had no choice but to confront their fear, which eventually was revealed to be Jesus himself.

BODY: What do you do?

✤ Considering the symbolism of the boat, the night, the wind and the spiritual presence that evoked first fear and then awe, how do you interpret the account in Matthew 14 of Jesus walking on the water?

✤ We all know that true courage is not in being fearless but in facing our fears. Whom do you admire for their courage? Who is your hero or heroine?

✤ Do you suffer from sensations of fear, caused by a person, a situation or a phobia? Could you seek help in addressing this fear and redirecting some of the energy it absorbs into your own healing?

✤ What is your reaction to the statement in John 4:18? 'There is no fear in love. But perfect love drives out fear, because fear has to do with punishment. The one who fears is not made perfect in love.' In the light of your response, what meaning does the common exhortation to 'fear the Lord!' have?

SPIRIT: Meanings

Fear is one of the deepest of emotions. It can bypass our intellect and our sense of what is right, and hit directly at our guts. There is nothing weak about experiencing fear. Jesus himself, kneeling in the Garden of Gethsemane, waiting for his arrest, sweated the blood of those who face death. He knew the sense of dread, of horror of what was to come, and he faced it alone while his disciples slept. He had known for some time that he must face this ordeal; it is hard to imagine what psychological stress a man in that position would be under, yet he kept his self-control. We too meet fear. Sometimes we are so moved it is almost impossible to control our own bodies. How we meet fear depends on our circumstances, yet until we face our fears they continue to haunt us. Maybe Jesus told us to pray for our enemies because in so doing we might eventually come to replace fear with love, a transition that seems as impossible as walking on water, yet one that Jesus managed, even on the cross.

PRAYER

Lord Jesus, when I feel afraid, I remember your courage;
when I feel helpless, I see you nailed, immovable, to a beam of wood.
When I sense my instinct to run is overriding my sense of what is right,
help me stand firm.
Replace my fear with love, replace my fear with peace.

'... the sheep listen to his voice. He calls his own sheep by name
and leads them out.' (NIV)

— John 10:3 See also Psalm 23, Luke 15:3, Mark 6:34

MIND: Food for thought

SHEEP IN THE BRITISH ISLES have become somewhat devalued of late and have been rather typecast in the victim role. Let's think about Palestinian sheep instead. These were quite another matter, being relatively intelligent and hardy, having to walk considerable distances to find pasture. Palestinian sheep were not guided by fear of dogs but by familiarity with the shepherd. They were not driven but followed, responding to the shepherd's voice. For such a sheep to have become lost, it must have wandered into a place where it could not hear the voice, or into a place where it was trapped and unable to help itself. There is a significant difference between following the flock in bewilderment, letting a dog push you around, and listening, with a degree of autonomy, for someone you know and trust. In biblical Palestine, if two flocks mingled, which often happened if a field or a fold was shared, the shepherd needed only to call and his own animals would separate out from the others.

In biblical culture, sheep were highly valued, providing many essential products. Shepherds were prepared to risk their lives to protect the flock from predators. It is no coincidence that lambs were one of the main sacrificial victims, for people gave what was precious to God.

BODY: What do you do?

❖ When are you a follower, going with the crowd?

❖ When do you become the shepherd, leading others?

❖ Do you ever drive others by barking and snapping at them until they go your way out of fear?

❖ Does your voice inspire the kind of trust that makes others follow you?

❖ Do you ever play the victim card? Why?

❖ In your response to God, are you more worried about following the rest of the flock, or listening out for the voice of the shepherd for yourself?

SPIRIT: Meanings

JESUS CALLED HIMSELF the good shepherd, presumably meaning one who leads, protects and guides; one who cares about each and every animal. Even when we walk in the darkest of valleys and feel the miserable weight of our own iniquity and weakness, still we are not worthless, and we are not completely lost. Our worst sins are forgiven and we are brought back to the fold, again and again. Jesus made no comment about the foolishness of the sheep, but only showed acceptance of its inherent nature and delight at its return. We may not feel we are worth the trouble, but God wants us to accept our rescue.

PRAYER

Dear Shepherd,
Teach me, the least of your lost lambs.
Teach me to know your voice above all others,
that my confusion might be replaced with confidence in you.
How often do I stray from your way?
Yet even so you reach out,
calling and searching endlessly
until I am safe with you again.

'You will tread on the lion and the adder, the young lion and the serpent
you will trample under foot. Those who love me, I will deliver;
I will protect those who know my name.' — Psalm 91:3–14 (NRSV)

MIND: Food for thought

I N THE CREATION MYTH of Genesis, Yahweh was angry with Eve for trusting the serpent instead of obeying his rule not to touch the forbidden fruit, and as a consequence invoked a terrible curse. The snake became the image of enmity between human and creature, a memorial to the conflict of deceit and innocence, of the power of manipulation over ignorance. The God Yahweh of the Old Testament was often portrayed as angry, and the cause was often the behaviour of the people he had attached himself to. They vacillated between fidelity and disloyalty throughout their history, frequently tempted away as though to some other forbidden fruit by the gruesome fertility cults of Canaan. The snake became linked to this vacillating faith in Numbers 21, where the wandering Hebrews were punished for complaining about living conditions by a plague of poisonous snakes. They repented that they had spoken against God and he then provided a remedy in the surprising form of a bronze snake. All they had to do was look on this in faith to be cured of a bite. The bronze snake was a sign demanding a faith-response, despite confusion and adversity. In order to be helped, the Israelites were being asked to demonstrate the faith they had previously held in derision.

BODY: What do you do?

HOW CONSTANT is your love of God? Does it vacillate depending on adversity or good fortune? Do you complain bitterly one minute and then want help the next?

✤ Do you ever feel your fidelity to God is being put to the test? What do you make of the statement in Exodus 34:14 that the Lord is a jealous God?

✤ For the ancient Israelites, Yahweh provided a bronze image to gaze upon. What antidote to poison do you need? What would jolt you into being healed?

✤ What things or people try to seduce you away from the true love of your life? How easily are you taken in? What defence do you have?

SPIRIT: Meanings

JESUS REFERRED TO THE BRONZE SERPENT in John 3:14, drawing a parallel between the snake being lifted up and the need for the 'Son of Man' to be lifted up so that all who believe may have eternal life. Maybe there is a connection with the words of Hosea 6:1–3, 'Come, let us return to the Lord, for it is he who has torn and he will heal us … after three days he will raise us up.' Hosea likened Israel's infidelity to the infidelity of his own wife. He connected his wish for reconciliation with the ultimately forgiving nature of God. The New Testament portrays God not as a God of wrath but of love. It is not fear but love that the Lord seeks, and as the quotation above expresses, God will do great things because of that love. While our fidelity, our love, may sometimes be tested, while our mystical 'marriage' may sometimes feel under great strain, God demands single-minded loyalty. When we can manage such confidence, despite even the venomous bite of snakes, then we are rewarded and our love comes back to us manifold.

PRAYER

Lord, give me reason to love you,
give me knowledge of your presence to strengthen my resolve.
When I weaken, be there to strengthen me,
lest in falling away I lose myself.

'It is out of the abundance of the heart
that the mouth speaks.' (NRSV)
— Luke 6:45

MIND: Food for thought

THE SQUIRREL that features in European folklore is the red squirrel, pine-tree lover. The larger and bolder grey squirrel was brought over from America in the 19th century. Purists disapprove of the grey squirrel and hold it responsible for the decline of the indigenous population of reds, although apparently this is not entirely justified. In the rather brutal Norse mythology centred around the Yggdrasil, the sacred world tree, there was a squirrel called Ratatosk who took messages (mainly threats and insults) between an all-seeing and all-knowing eagle at the top and a snake gnawing at the roots. In between was the level where people lived. The ability of the squirrel to leap and climb with such agility gave rise to the symbolism of communication, and although we might not wish to communicate with the beings respected by the Vikings, we might pursue the symbolism of the squirrel as go-between. The Vikings made the squirrel a gossip-monger and a trouble-maker, which is the negative aspect of communication. That leaves us free to claim the positive side, which brings us into the realm of angels, true messengers of God.

BODY: What do you do?

THE WRITER OF THE GOSPEL of Matthew, sternly protecting the timelessness of the law and the need for personal righteousness, records Jesus as warning that by our words we will be condemned. We shall be obliged to account for every careless word we utter on the day of judgement (Matthew 12:36). How do you feel about this?

❖ Are you ever like mischievous Ratatosk, spreading trouble?

❖ Are you ever an anti-Ratatosk, spreading oil on troubled waters as a peacemaker?

❖ Do you ever feel uneasy that you have said too much, or not enough?

❖ In what ways do you normally communicate with God? How do you pray?

❖ In what ways have you felt that God communicates with you?

SPIRIT: Meanings

THE CHURCH IN HISTORY, I believe, condoned the belief that chattering at God through the wordiness of liturgies is helpful, while it did little to improve inadequate provision for education. Its insistence in the past that priests were essential as go-betweens between the laity and a remote God echoes the function of Ratatosk. The fact that Christians were imprisoned for claiming the right to be in direct communication with God is shocking to us now, but highlights the importance of the struggle to claim the right to individual spiritual experience. We have that right – in fact we are incomplete without it. We also have the right to find our own way of being with God, for this in essence is what prayer is. It doesn't matter what we say, nor does God notice our rituals. They are done for our sake, to assist our own meditation, or they are worthless. God knows the language of the heart. Our words need to be in harmony with that impulse.

PRAYER

Teach me to live out my prayer
in every heartbeat, every thought, every feeling.
Teach me to find not words, but harmony with you.

'My brothers and sisters, do you with your acts of favouritism really believe in our glorious Lord Jesus Christ? … Have you not made distinctions among yourselves and become judges with evil thoughts?' — James 2:1& 4 (NRSV)

MIND: Food for thought

THE SPARROW represents the smallest and humblest of creatures; it is not only dowdy in appearance but also common. Sparrows are the plain and ordinary, those who are apparently unremarkable in every way but exist in little flocks with their chattering friends, always around the same modest territory. Swallows, in comparison, are spectacular in their mastery of the air, more streamline, more striking, tiny travellers of astonishing distances. We might look with envy as they mass on the telegraph wires ready to leave for warmer climates, while we steel ourselves for the onset of winter. It may seem strange at first that two such different birds are coupled together. They appear both in the biblical wisdom sayings of Proverbs (26:2) and in Psalm 84:3. The first reference, in Proverbs, contrasts the fluttering of sparrows with the darting of swallows and says that, likewise, an undeserved curse never comes to rest. The second reference says that the temple of God is so wonderful that even such different birds as these make their homes within it, close to the altar itself.

BODY: What do you do?

IT IS EASY TO BE SEDUCED by the jet-setting lifestyle. It's easy to look down on those who seem left behind, those who seem so dull. But it is not our business to judge others, nor is it our place to assume their priorities are the same as ours. Swallows and sparrows receive the same love from God and it is our task to be channels of this love.

❖ Jesus said that the measure we use to judge others will be applied to ourselves (Matthew 7:1). When you make comments about others, do you ever sense that the same might be true about yourself?

❖ Are you a swallow or a sparrow? Either way, you are free to nest in God's house. Do you make excuses to exclude yourself?

❖ Do you ever belittle people simply because they are not like you? Do you secretly believe in your own superiority? Or do you suffer from an inferiority complex?

❖ What about the people in your 'flock'? Do they support equanimity?

SPIRIT: Meanings

THESE TWO CONTRASTING BIRDS are used to encompass all humanity. Despite our differences, we still share enough characteristics to have common ground; we can always meet in the house of God, as we make our own homes there. It is significant that Matthew's and Luke's Gospels record Jesus as drawing attention to the sparrows without the swallows; according to Matthew not one sparrow will fall to the ground without the will of God, and according to Luke not one is forgotten. The passage goes on to say that the very hairs on our heads are numbered, such is the omniscience of God. That Jesus singled out sparrows is worth noting, for his entire ministry was directed towards such seemingly insignificant people. He wanted them to know that long ago the sparrows lived alongside the swallows in the house of God. He wanted them to know they were welcome back. But he also wanted people to stop making value judgements about each other based on appearances. The kingdom is for all and it is not our place to rank one above another.

PRAYER

Father God, in your house are many rooms. Even though I have judged others, have felt myself sometimes superior, sometimes inferior, and have looked unequally on others and made distinctions, still I hope to dwell with you, and with all, in peaceful community. Forgive me for the superficiality of my vision. Teach me to see with your eyes, to know that all are welcome.

'See, I am sending you out like sheep in the midst of wolves;
so be wise as serpents and innocent as doves.' (NRSV)
— Matthew 10:16. See also Isaiah 22:9, Isaiah 65:25

MIND: Food for thought

WOLVES FEATURE WIDELY IN THE BIBLE and in the folklore of the northern hemisphere. As predators they were much feared: the Saxons called the month of January Wolf-monath, or Wolf-month, as, according to Verstegan, this was the time when people and livestock were most likely to be eaten by wolves, ravenous after a long winter. Apparently though, where there is space to do so, wolves avoid humans and fulfil the necessary role of combing out the weak and struggling from among wild herds. It is argued that they are 'helpful' predators, and that we should respect the closeness of their matriarchal pack structure and the care they give their young. The writer of Isaiah 11:6 prophesied a time when 'a shoot shall come out from the stump of Jesse' (meaning a descendant of David's line) and bring such peace that 'the wolf shall live with the lamb, the leopard shall lie down with the kid …' He saw an end to destruction and hurt 'for the earth will be full of the knowledge of the Lord as the waters cover the sea'. The prophet's vision speaks of a time that Christians feel is associated with the presence of Christ, where even the naturally fierce will become gentle. It sounds too good to be true, but it is said, after all, that with God all things are possible (Matthew 19:26).

BODY: What do you do?

THINK OF TIMES when you have sensed hostility from another. How did you react? Is there pain, humiliation, confusion or anger still with you? Do you need to hold on to it still, or are you ready to seek healing? Have you brought the pain into your prayers?

✤ Read John 14:27: 'Peace I leave with you, my peace I give to you … do not let your hearts be troubled, and do not let them be afraid.' How might you find this peace? Have you asked for it? What do you contribute to the spread of peace, so that wolves might indeed live with lambs?

✤ Jesus told us to pray for our enemies; even to love them. How do you feel about this?

✤ Do you feel that forgiveness helps the healing process?

✤ When you see people who have been hurt by human violence, what is your instinctive reaction?

SPIRIT: Meanings

JESUS SAID there would be predators looking for a kill, and prayed to God that his followers would be protected (John 17:11). He warned that there were risks in following him and showed by his own example the depth of courage required to stay true to the message of God. He also told us what to do about such enemies. Instead of hating them, which is the natural reaction, and very much the prevalent sentiment found in the Old Testament, Jesus told us to love them, and pray for those who persecute us (Matthew 5:43–47). It is not until we have been hurt that we realise how hard this can be. It takes a long time to deal with the shock-waves of uncertainty, anger, shame, bitterness and fear, and the word forgiveness can almost sound like betrayal of self-respect. Yet Jesus was crucified and still could find the voice to pray, 'Father, forgive them, for they do not know what they are doing.' Maybe the best we can do is pray for the strength to repeat that same prayer.

PRAYER

Christ who forgave your killers,
teach me to pray for those who seem set against me.
Give me your peace, that my heart may be untroubled.
Give me your peace that I may not be afraid.

FEATURES OF THE NATURAL WORLD

'In him we live and move and have our being.' (NIV)
— Acts 17:28

MIND: Food for thought

WITHOUT AIR, of course, we cannot live. All life is dependent on the Earth's unique atmosphere; elementary biology lessons teach us how each plant and creature breathes in its own way; how the forests cleanse our air, how fish gills work, how blood transports oxygen and carbon dioxide in a constant cycle. We know about aerobic exercise and the benefits of relaxed, calm breathing; we know that aeroplanes are safe because invisible forces support them as they fly. Considering how wonderful the air is, it is surprising how much we take it for granted. It is even more surprising how we pollute it and condone its pollution; by poisoning the air we are poisoning ourselves. I remember walking one summer evening on Hampstead Heath, which seemed green and pleasant enough, and looking over towards the city of London. Above the sprawling grey of brick and stone was a brown haze. I had a sudden feeling of concern for the people living in this smog; I wished I could bring some clean woodland air to them. In air, whatever its quality, we live and move and have our being. We can see our dependence on air as an analogy for our relationship with God.

BODY: What do you do?

DEEP BREATHING is relaxing and empowering. So too is deep prayer. Several religions have developed ways of praying that focus on the breath, or the repetition of a word or short phrase that regularises the breathing. Simply feeling the presence of God rushing in and our own poison flowing out is a powerful meditation that can replace words. Shallow breathing is associated with fear. In spiritual terms it is as though we are afraid to make contact with God. We can utter shallow prayers, we can avoid empowerment, but why should we want to?

❖ Do you breathe deeply of God? Or do you avoid true prayer?

❖ Why might you deprive yourself of the empowerment you need? What is your fear?

❖ Try different ways of praying that focus on the sacred breath.

SPIRIT: Meanings

IT IS REASSURING to know that God is incorruptible and that, despite the poison of our own minds, Spirit remains pure. We cannot pollute God; we can only recognise our own pollution. When we meditate on the all-pervasive quality of air, we can see an even deeper truth – that God too is simultaneously within us and all around us. Just as air unites all life, God is One. God is within you and me, whether we acknowledge the Presence or not, and we can live our lives as active prayers. While we already live continuously in God, like a fish who never leaves the water, we can and should make time to focus specifically on this awe-inspiring truth. In our prayer life we need to be like a surfacing seal filling its lungs ready for another dive. It is the vital time we take to replenish ourselves, to cleanse and renew. It is the means by which we gain the strength we need to meet life. Without it life is shallow and superficial; with it we are empowered.

PRAYER

Lord of Life, let me breathe deeply
of your Spirit,
that my life may become a living prayer,
my thoughts ever mindful of your empowering presence.

'Take care that you do not despise one of these little ones; for, I tell you, in heaven their angels continually see the face of my Father in heaven.' (NRSV)
— Matthew 18:10. See also Exodus 23:21

MIND: Food for thought

ANGELS FEATURE PROMINENTLY in the art and literature of early Christianity, including the carvings and knotwork of the Celtic Church. Calm, wide-eyed beings watch us from old walls and illuminated manuscripts, timeless faces, still communicating their own sanctity today. There is of course frequent mention of angels in the Bible. Sometimes in the Old Testament we read of an angel, sometimes the angel of the Lord, and by the time of the Book of Daniel, we can read about angels with names and personalities such as Gabriel. In the New Testament, the Greek word *angelos*, meaning messenger, was used to translate the Hebrew *mal'ak*. Both words would normally be understood as referring to a spiritual being, immaterial, ethereal, a power rather than a body, an emanation of God acting as a mouth-piece and agent. There are also instances where the word refers to a human messenger bringing a divine message. While modern minds might struggle to accept the reality of white-robed, flying beings, the concept of angels has by no means become out of date. God is not limited in choice of messengers: we may receive divine communication in any form we are prepared to accept; the only complication is in being able to discern which messages we receive are divinely inspired, and which have arisen from a lower state of self-interest.

BODY: What do you do?

THE DIFFICULTY many people have with angels is that they do not move their thinking on from primary school nativity plays and tinsel-clad, winged children. To think seriously about such entities we need to forget we have ever seen such displays! The Bible, not the infant teacher responsible for costume, is the true authority on angels.

❖ Do you dismiss the concept of angels along with Father Christmas and the Tooth Fairy, or have you ever felt that it is worth pursuing the possibility in a more adult context?

❖ Or do you believe in angels while also believing in the existence of other supernatural beings or phenomena that are not attested to in the Bible?

❖ Have you traced all the references to angels in the Old and New Testaments? It is a subject worthy of study, both to gain insight into the spiritual thinking of ancient minds, and to deepen your awareness of the different biblical concepts that exist. Some may be more helpful to you than others.

SPIRIT: Meanings

I REMEMBER DISCUSSING ANGELS with a Muslim child of six, who told me that we all have two angels with us, sitting on either shoulder. Not only are they there to guide and protect us, they also remind us to be sensitive to the angels accompanying others, lest we shock them in any way. The idea had great influence on this little girl, who was – and still is – one of the most sparkling, radiant and poetic beings I have met. While I would not claim that children are angels as such, they are certainly more open to acting on impulse, maybe sometimes an impulse from God. Once, as I sat quietly in a church trying to wrestle with some moral dilemma in which I was entangled, doubtless worrying more than praying, I felt a pat on the knee. The three-year-old son of my companions solemnly gave me a card he had just picked up from the back of the church, bearing the words of St Augustine: 'Trust the past to the mercy of God, the present to his love and the future to his providence.' To me, that was enough of a spiritual nudge to feel very certain that some messenger of God was very close.

PRAYER

Father, teach me to be not childish but childlike in my openness to you.
When you send your messengers to me, let me receive them gladly.
May your angels guard me and watch over me.

*'Can any of you by worrying add a single hour
to your span of life?'* (NRSV)
— Matthew 6:27

MIND: Food for thought

BUBBLES ARE PART OF THE DELIGHT of childhood and they contain a lesson that almost any little child can teach you. The bubble exists only in the present. The moment it pops, it is in the past, gone. You cannot get that bubble back, you can only blow a new one. So too, life. We have only the present moment. All else has gone, or exists only as speculation. Many of our anxieties are caused by fantasies about the various future scenarios that we do not want to happen. Many of those scenarios are based on events that belong in the past. As adults we become very good at drawing from the past to make images of the future, and this is the way we spend our present moments. In other words we waste them by worrying, when we don't need to. The immediacy of a bubble, the entrancing delicacy, the perfect wholeness, the fluid, rainbow-filled membrane, these are things to marvel at while they are there in front of you.

BODY: What do you do?

WHAT THOUGHTS DO YOU HAVE about the distant future, the next week, the next day and hour? Do you have it all mapped out? Is there one event that is absorbing all your thoughts? Under what circumstances is it appropriate to invest a high level of mental energy in an event in the future?

✤ How do you react to the suggestion that all your thoughts about the future are as yet pipe dreams and fantasies?

✤ How much do you dwell on the past? Do you wish it would go away? Can you let it go away? If not, why do you have to hold on to it? If you are not enjoying the memory, where can you seek healing?

✤ Do you ever put the past and the future in God's hands so that you can enjoy the present?

SPIRIT: Meanings

BUBBLES NOT ONLY CONTAIN the lesson of immediacy and living to enjoy the present moment, they contain rainbows. Rainbows are the delight of children and those who have found their child-at-heart. Rainbows contain the promise of grace, of God's unconditional love and acceptance of us. Grace too belongs to children; on the whole, they are the only ones who know how to accept it, for they have no choice, they are not responsible for anything. Children (usually) know that they are loved uncon-ditionally, despite all the trouble they get into; they know that, whatever happens, they can find comfort with a loving parent who is so big they can help find a way through the tears and the problems until everyone is happy again. A child who does not know this is a hurt child who needs healing before they become a damaged adult. Bubbles are messages to know God's love now, before the moment is gone!

PRAYER

Mother God, you who delight with me in the wonders of the instant,
I would rid my mind of fantasies and fears,
so that I might see beauty where before I saw nothing of value,
so that I might learn from children how to live happily and be loved.

'Yet O Lord, you are our Father. We are the clay, you are the potter;
we are all the work of your hand.' (NIV)

— Isaiah 64:8. See also Job 10:9, 33:6, Isaiah 29:16

MIND: Food for thought

CLAY, TO READ BETWEEN THE LINES of the Old Testament, was a cheap, plentiful and invaluable natural resource, with multifarious uses. These included producing disposable vessels essential for the cleanliness rituals; sealing interior and exterior walls; and making moulds for the casting of bronze objects, tablets for writing, bricks and sturdy jars used for storing important documents. Its malleability was referred to by prophets, likewise the ease with which it could be reduced to dust. Ezekiel was even told by God to draw pictures and model in clay, to demonstrate a prophecy (Ezekiel 4:1). For Job or Isaiah to state that we are like clay was not so much to marvel in the creative potential of the material, as a modern potter might relish the prospect of forming a unique work of art. It was a statement of ordinariness. Clay was literally dirt-cheap and if God the potter didn't like the way a pot was coming out he could simply reshape it. Not only are we ordinary, shaped from the dust and soon to return to dust, we are also brittle, fragile and impermanent.

BODY: What do you do?

HAVE YOU WORKED WITH CLAY? It is a very therapeutic and satisfying medium, one I have frequently used with emotionally unsettled children. It does not necessarily matter to them that they have made a pot but they are normally very pleased to have thoroughly beaten out all the air pockets!

❖ In what ways do you exercise the divine gift of creativity to make useful products?

❖ How do you deal with the statement 'dust to dust'? Does it chill you, or do you sense the rightness of the regenerative cycle?

SPIRIT: Meanings

I HAVE A DISTANT MEMORY of an old lady gardener amazing me once as a little girl when I went to 'help'. She said, 'You know why we have to look after the earth? See, we belong to it!' And she put down her spade, spat and rubbed her hands together to show me how dark soil appeared. At the time it looked as though she was rubbing away her own skin and that she was made of the earth. I know I tried it too and my hands were so grubby that I could see for myself that I too was made of soil! Only later did I discover the wider truth that the whole of our planet is made from interchangeable particles that originated from the explosions of stars. We do belong to the earth, we belong to the universe. Considering the marvel of this fact, we have no right, as Isaiah reminds us, to belittle our own fragile existence or that of any other: 'Do you question me about my children, or give me orders about the work of my hands?' (Isaiah 45:11) What God had breathed life on, we are to respect, for we all come from the same star dust and to star dust do we return.

PRAYER

Lord of Life,
You who flung the stars out into the darkness,
grant me a sense of perspective
that I may sense awe and humility before your creation.

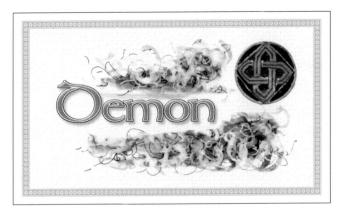

'Jesus answered, "I do not have a demon; but I honour my Father,
and you dishonour me."' (NRSV)
— John 8:49. See also Matthew 12:28

MIND: Food for thought

MUCH MISCHIEF was attributed to demons in the theology of both Testaments. They were reputed to be the cause of certain types of illness, a force in opposition to God, influencing the minds of helpless people. Some claim that God is a construct of human consciousness at a higher level; yet it seems more likely to me that it is the demons who are the result of human thought and activity. They are a projection of fear, hatred and self-interest. They are absence of God. They have power only because they are worshipped by so many. When our hearts beat in time not with the love of God but with hatred, then we forget God, and trouble is born. A demon does not need a physical embodiment; it is entirely unhelpful to connect the concept with images of Pan for example. To give shape to our fear simply gives it more weight, more substance. Yet what real power can a 'demon' have? I suspect only the power that we give it. The old belief was that demons, as though they had independent existence, took possession of unwitting people. But a demon is not like a parasite; it cannot hop from one host to another. It is not like a goblin that scuttles around causing trouble. To believe this is to deny responsibility for our own minds. A demon is the product of a malevolent thought, one that might bring self-harm as easily as harm of others; it is a thought that festers and grows, because the thinker allows it oxygen to thrive. As it grows it multiplies, and its effects are soon noticed. It is as though that person has relinquished control to an evil power, yet that power originated from within their own corrupt thought. We do not fall prey to demons, we create them in our moments of Godlessness.

BODY: What do you do?

WHEN HAVE YOU BLAMED something external to yourself for your own actions? In retrospect, for which of these instances could you have admitted some responsibility?

❖ What demons might you have given life to?

❖ What is your view on the dualistic theory that there is a battle between the forces of good and evil?

❖ How do you know when you can rely on a book that purports to give information about Jesus? How important is it to find out what he really thought and did? How much do you model Jesus according to your own views?

❖ How literally do you take the Gospel accounts of demons being cast out? Would you seek a modern medical or psychological explanation for most of the cases? If not, how do you interpret illness today?

SPIRIT: Meanings

SOME RELIGIONS centre around the concept of a battle between good and evil. This dualistic belief was popular among some gnostic sects within the early church, and also with the Essenes, a Jewish sect practising at the time of Jesus. Some like to claim that Jesus himself was an Essene. While he seems to have had trusted friends within the group, his own teachings recorded in the gospels do not reflect the same beliefs. Jesus did not believe there was a threat to God's supremacy; he saw the kingdom of God as supreme. God's presence is that which shines through when the tarnish of destructive thoughts is wiped away. The corrosion requires cleansing and restoration. This is the task Jesus undertook. Thus, when he was accused of having a demon himself, even of working in the name of Beelzebub, prince of demons, he retorted that this was impossible, and that his work was through the Spirit of God, which brought the kingdom of God to the people (Matthew 12:28).

PRAYER

Lord, you acted in the power of the Spirit of God,
to bring the kingdom of heaven to earth.
Show me my own demons, and set me free from their influence,
that I might be renewed and healed.

'And just as he was coming up out of the water, he saw the heavens torn apart
and the Spirit descending like a dove on him … And the Spirit immediately
drove him out into the wilderness.' — Mark 1:10 & 12 (NRSV)

MIND: Food for thought

BIRDS ARE BLESSED among creatures in their ability to travel the three realms of air, earth and water; in their flight they commune with the wind, ancient symbol of the Spirit's movement. There is a word in Hebrew for this wind-like presence of God: *ruah*. Ruah comes from a word meaning to breathe out strongly, and came to mean the animating principle, that which brought life and vitality, originating from God. It occurs for example in Genesis 1:2, as a 'wind from God', sweeping over the waters, at the start of the creation narrative. Several birds have entered into the domain of sacred symbolism, drawing on this close association between wild, free movement and the wind. We might be reminded of the power in Isaiah's song of praise: 'But those who hope in the Lord will renew their strength. They will soar on wings like eagles; they will run and not grow weary …' (Isaiah 40:31) Or again we might think of the presence of the Spirit at Jesus's baptism, said to come down 'as a dove'. In the Celtic tradition, the wild goose came to be seen in a similar way: the ancient saints perceived the goose as a symbol of the untamed nature of the Spirit. Feather also speaks of the wind that supports seemingly effortless flight. A wild bird has a freedom that no earth-bound creature has. The Spirit too is not governed by space and time; her power is free and unconstrained. Our own spiritual quest is like a struggle to break free, so that we too can rise up with wings like eagles, and suddenly see everything in a different way.

BODY: What do you do?

WHEN WE HAVE LEARNED TO FLY on the wind of the Spirit, grace fills every task and every responsibility so that we are no longer weighed down. If we feel that we simply cannot soar in spiritual freedom then perhaps it is time to take flight in a different way from whatever is tying us down, whether it is our own fear or external pressures. For what is more saddening than the sight of a wild bird shut in a cage?

❧ What, or who, is it that you feel ties you down?

❧ How free are you? And how free do you really want to be? Do you find it unnerving to think that the Spirit might lead you anywhere? Maybe it is not freedom but security that we seek. What do you think? Can we feel secure in God?

SPIRIT: Meanings

PARADOXICALLY, spiritual freedom is the consequence of handing over power to God. The feather is a symbol of freedom from the weight of guilt and worry. The vision of a bird in flight should be incentive enough to throw everything to the wind, so that we might be lifted up above the busy world to see with a new clarity. But above all, Spirit is the dynamic force that compels us to move on, to grow, to change, and to find new life. It demands freedom to lay down our nets and follow the call wherever it leads us. The first thing the Spirit, 'as a dove', did to Jesus immediately after his baptism was to drive or compel him into the wilderness (Mark 1:9–13). The Spirit is not just about feeling 'enthusiastic'; it forces us to face ourselves in honesty, and it compels us to search for God, sometimes in the most unexpected places.

PRAYER

Holy Spirit, free me from the ties that constrain,
free me from the troubles that ensnare,
lift me up that I might fly
with wings like an eagle's
that I may run where you choose and not grow weary or afraid.

'... For this reason I remind you to fan into flame the gift of God, which is in you through the laying on of my hands. For God did not give us a spirit of timidity, but a spirit of power, of love and of self-discipline.' — 2 Timothy 1:6–7 (NIV)

MIND: Food for thought

A PROMISE WAS MADE, long ago, that the Spirit of Truth would be sent to us as our comforter and advocate, the means by which many wonderful deeds might take place (John 14:17). In fulfilment of the promise, the early followers of Christ received the gift of the Spirit, which came like tongues of fire to enlighten them (Acts 2:1–12). The candle flame is a reminder of that promise; it represents the energy of the Spirit amongst us. We cannot hold this Spirit of Truth or confine it, we can only be held. But true insight is constantly moving and expanding, dynamic and free. Like fire it needs fuel to grow and move on. Given the freedom to explore, it will devour every fragment of dry, dead matter within. One spark of the truth is enough to burn down our every preconception and assumption. It has the power to strip us of everything we thought we knew, everything we believed to be right. Fire, given total freedom, is relentless. But nature is big enough to accept fire; it is part of the vital process of regeneration. After fire, the land is enriched and new seeds have room to grow. Life returns, invigorated.

BODY: What do you do?

WE SHOULD NEVER ASSUME that we have the whole Truth, for fire is hungry for growth. We should never allow ourselves to take fire for granted, or lapse into a false sense of security.

❖ Have you ever told God that you are looking for 'the truth'? If so, what happened next, or are you still waiting?

❖ Do you see value in investigating the real Jesus, or is it enough to believe in the Christ of faith? Does historicity and theological study threaten your faith? Do you believe that having an open mind remains important in the sphere of your personal faith?

❖ In my theological studies, over a decade ago, there was one major religion not available on the syllabus; the University apparently could not find a scholar of that faith who was prepared to treat the scripture objectively or analytically. What would your response be to this situation?

SPIRIT: Meanings

IT SEEMS that the ancient Israelites had an uneasy relationship with this power that at once warmed and fed them, but at the same time threatened to destroy all they had. If we equate fire with the Spirit of Truth, we have to recognise that Truth can indeed be terrifying. Once dare to seek the Truth and we unleash an awe-inspiring energy, a baptism of fire. But the fire is a gift of the Spirit; it will cleanse us and renew us. Anyone who has the courage to seek the real Truth will in time come to appreciate what effect the search has. Jesus spoke of the chaff being burnt out in 'unquenchable fire'. We can lose our chaff without being destroyed, for at our heart is a precious seed. The Truth does indeed set free, but we must respect the awesome power of the Spirit. Like love, as described in the Song of Solomon, perhaps truth too should only be stirred up when we are ready to listen to its message.

PRAYER

Holy Spirit,
Teach me to welcome the unquenchable fire
that will burn up my chaff and leave me pure.
Prepare me for the baptism you bring,
that I may recognise your voice of Truth.

'Rabbi, who sinned, this man or his parents, that he was born blind?' Jesus answered,
'Neither this man nor his parents sinned; he was born blind so that God's works
might be revealed in him.' — John 9:1 (NRSV)

MIND: Food for thought

THE FLOOD features in the Bible as one of the primary terrors faced by humans, along with fire, drought, plague and warfare. In ancient times, natural events were always interpreted in the context of divine action, whether beneficial or harmful. The Bible is full of disasters, which are normally seen as punishments, but there are also beneficial events, which are seen as blessings. In fact everything out of the immediate control of people was placed in the hands of God, from the weather to the success of the harvest, from a woman's capacity for childbirth to the onset of illness. Now we know the physical reasons why most things of this nature happen, and we can explain misfortune without needing to link it all to our moral and religious behaviour; in fact it has now become repugnant to suggest that victims of disasters are anything but innocent. So we need to look carefully at our concept of God and our relationship with God. For if we hold the ancient idea of reward and punishment too dear, we fall into the regrettable position of condemning those we see suffering, like Job's friends, who assumed that he must have sinned to have brought such trouble upon himself. Jesus, in the quotation above, and also in Luke 13, began the process of turning the whole idea around. He replaced the idea of God punishing the individual with the new and very positive idea of an opportunity for healing.

BODY: What do you do?

READ THE PARABLE of the wise man who built on rock and the foolish man who built on loose sand (Matthew 7:26). Here is a description of a disaster: a man's house falls down. Where is God in this story? Does God send the flood? No, it just happens. Is there any mention of punishment? No. Is God in the wisdom of the first man, who understood enough about soil mechanics to avoid building in the sand of the riverbank? The parable is not a lesson in punishment; it is a lesson in building on firm foundations, namely the teachings of Jesus. In this way we gain the wisdom we need to face life, even the threat of flood waters. Following Jesus, even if the floods do rise against us, we can be confident that they are not meant as a personal attack, but are part of the natural world. Our role is to seek God's help in rising above adversity and through it gain new strength.

SPIRIT: Meanings

WE NEED TO LOOK at the consequences of believing in a God who uses natural events as a way of rewarding and punishing. We need to look at what we can believe about God's interaction with us. The reward/punishment concept is one way of parenting, which fits the covenant concept of Israel as the children of God. But it is not the only way of bringing up children. A more child-centred approach might be reward/help, or reward/support. A parent should not cause unmitigated suffering for their child's misdemeanours. Anyone these days following the advice on disciplining children of Proverbs 23:13, 'If you beat them with a rod, they will not die,' would quite rightly be tried for child abuse. Parents do their best to help the child see through their difficulties. We should not blame God when hard times strike, or assume that we are being punished for something. We should turn to God for help, for only then can we hope to make sense of the turmoil and the distress.

PRAYER

Loving Father, let me not see you as a remote controller, constantly pulling strings to cause one event after another. The earth, the universe, is unfolding in its own way, just as I am, and has been doing since the beginning of time. You watch it change and grow, and you are there with us when the huge processes of the earth affect our lives. Teach me not to blame you but to ask you for help in the way I react. When I, who am so small, cannot change events that are so big, let me at least find strength and understanding in your wisdom; let me seek opportunities for healing.

'All this I have tested by wisdom: I said, "I will be wise," but it was far from me.
That which is, is far off, and deep, very deep; who can find it out?' (NRSV)
— Ecclesiastes 7:23

MIND: Food for thought

THE EFFECTS OF WINTER must have been felt so much more harshly in days gone by, days without double glazing and central heating, without electric lights and waterproofs. The winter is harsh, the animals know and hibernate, yet we struggle on, starved of daylight, huddled in thick layers, waiting for a sign of spring. When the water freezes, today our main concern is with the state of our pipes and ice on the roads. But for a people who had to fetch their own water, there must have been added hardship. Now, for most of us, winter is simply an uncomfortable inconvenience. For those more at the mercy of the environment, it can be a real test of survival. We can – and do – experience such times in our spiritual lives, when it feels we are making no progress, that a fog separates us from the sun, from the light we seek. It is as though we live and move in darkness and half-light, dejected and run-down, cold, and forgetful of the warmth and vibrancy that is spring. It is as though God is distant and we have only our own poor, depleted energy to rely on. Yet spring does come and so too do our periods of spiritual standstill pass away.

BODY: What do you do?

I N THE SUMMER it is hard to remember the hostility of winter; in winter it is equally hard to imagine sunbathing in the garden. When we are on a spiritual 'roll' it is easy to be bowled along and forget that there are times when everything seems harder. A fable of Aesop tells of a lazy grasshopper who made no preparation for winter and then suffered the consequences. Our times of spiritual richness are times to build up strength and insight, as a support and a comfort when we start to struggle. Otherwise, we travel along on a spiritual roller-coaster, completely unable to stop the ceaseless ups and downs.

* What 'evidence' can you accumulate for yourself of your own spiritual insight, to restore your hope in times of hardship?
* Can you bring greater stability into the progress of your spiritual develop-ment, with fewer extremes between ice and ecstasy? Would a figurative move nearer to the equator mean that you were more constantly in the presence of the 'sun'?

SPIRIT: Meanings

W E CAN SYMPATHISE with the sense of failure the disciples of Jesus must have felt when they unsuccessfully attempted to heal a child in Jesus's absence (Matthew 17:14–20). It must have hurt to feel God was not helping. The feeling of abandonment was understood by Jesus but also addressed by him. The solution to the disciples' difficulty was not in trying to force God's will and work magic, even for the good of another. The solution was to pray and to allow even a speck of faith, even a grain of hope, that this request might be in accord with God's will. The point at which spring starts to arrive and the ice melts is the point at which we acknowledge that it is not we who have the power to bring healing, life and renewal. These gifts come quite naturally from a power beyond ourselves, a power infinitely greater and wiser, in which we can trust, but through which we must also learn patience. The truth is that even in winter growth and life continue – but within. Buds wait at the tips of branches, lambs exist as embryos. Not all growth is outwardly visible.

PRAYER

Lord, on the cross you touched the loneliness of feeling forsaken by God.
Yet you were not forsaken, you were drawn through and beyond the pain,
through your own winter and on into the glory of spring.
Be with me in my own winters, draw me through the darkness
and on to rediscover light and life.

*'When I look at your heavens, the work of your fingers, the moon and the stars
that you have established; what are human beings that you are mindful of them,
mortals, that you care for them?'* — Psalm 8:3–4 (NRSV)

MIND: Food for thought

THE MOON, in her journeying, describes a vast circle around our Earth, and while her journey is constant and uninterrupted, we perceive it as a cycle of ever-changing phases. Although the moon is simply a huge sphere of rock, we see sometimes a crescent, sometimes a semicircle, sometimes nothing at all. What awe this cycle must have inspired in ancient minds can only be imagined. We know that the moon was worshipped as a god by some ancient cultures. The town of Ur, which Abraham left behind, has been shown by archaeologists to have been the centre of a moon-worshipping cult and one of the myths of that area names the consort of the moon god as Sarah. It is interesting that Abraham and Sarah walked away from this cult, so Genesis tells us, obedient to the voice of the Lord (Genesis 11:27–32). The moon's light is a further source of symbolism: its gentle glow is easy to gaze at; in fact to sit outside on a summer evening and watch the moon until you know it has moved a significant distance is a sure way to slow down time and still the mind. As you watch, think how people long ago did just the same thing; in fact even the dinosaurs watched the same moon, so long ago. How ancient life is! How small we are!

BODY: What do you do?

THE MOON DEMONSTRATES our relationship with God. Part of us faces God, part turns away. The cycle that we see represents the way we too wax and wane in our commitment to the spiritual life. Sometimes we grow, sometimes we shrink and the light seems to fade away, but then our hope returns again. We are always changing, moving on in a dance around our earth and our God.

❖ What quality of God would you most wish to reflect? Use the thought of this quality in your meditations.

❖ How do you react to the idea that isolation from God is felt simply when we turn our backs?

❖ Are you trying to shine with your own power? Where do you get your energy from if not from God?

SPIRIT: Meanings

THE MOON SHINES not with a power from within itself but with the reflected light of the sun. The light of the sun brings beauty to the face of the moon and gladness to the faces of people who seek a reassuring guide in the night. Our earth-eyes cannot gaze at the sun for its brilliance is blinding, but in the moon we see a gentler, softer light. So, too, we can become reflectors of our spiritual sun, the true source of our spiritual power. For just as the moon has no power of its own, neither do we. We need to reach the point where we are illuminated with the light of Spirit, having accepted that our own power is superficial. Unlike the light reflected by the moon, though, the Light of God shines not only from outside, from an external source, but also from within. If we do not reflect this Light and this Power then we reflect nothing – we are dull shadows, chilled like the shadow side of the moon.

PRAYER

Lord God, source of all light and life,
illuminate my heart and mind
that your light within me might shine through my eyes,
that your light outside me might be reflected in kindness on my face.

'After the earthquake came a fire, but the Lord was not in the fire. And after the fire came a gentle whisper. When Elijah heard it, he pulled his cloak over his face and went out and stood at the mouth of the cave.' — 1 Kings 19:12–13 (NIV)

MIND: Food for thought

MOUNTAINS have long been seen as an abode of the gods: a place to go to in seeking divine guidance, in offering worship, even sacrifice; a place where revelations might startle the unsuspecting traveller. Whether they are dark and rocky, snow-covered or densely forested, we instinctively feel awe. Those who venture to climb a great summit speak with respect and go well prepared to meet any eventuality. Experience engenders humility; there is no room for pride where a fall could cost a life. But there is also a passion in the heart of many a mountaineer, a deep-seated love of the challenge, a love of the wild, wide view, reaching far away into the horizon, a sense of great solitude and peace. An account in the Old Testament describes how Elijah, a greatly respected prophet of Yahweh, was compelled to go to a mountain 'for Yahweh will pass by'. Jesus too frequented the hills and mountains, choosing them as a place to go alone to pray. It is interesting that he chose a natural, wild place to go, exposed to the elements and creatures, free from the noise of human existence. It is also interesting that he is not described as seeking God in a conventional place of worship. Rather, he went to the synagogues to demonstrate the compassionate works of God, to teach and to talk with the leaders. His strength came to him in the solitude of the mountains, where he might spend a whole night alone in prayer under the stars. He then brought this strength down the mountain with him to make it accessible to others, to those caught up in the comfort and security of village and town life, who would never venture out alone to the wild places for fear of animals, robbers and the darkness itself.

BODY: What do you do?

SPIRITUAL EXPERIENCE comes to each of us a different way. There is little point in insisting that we will accept nothing short of a burning bush or an audible voice from nowhere. This leads to disillusionment. God does not bend to the limitations we try to impose; we need to stretch to accommodate the limitlessness of God.

❖ Have you ever felt the presence of God in nature?

❖ Elijah knew God was speaking when he heard a gentle whisper. Would you be as quick to recognise the voice of God, or do you wait to be shouted at?

❖ How do you visualise the progress you are making as you climb your mountain?

SPIRIT: Meanings

JESUS WAS NOT AFRAID to walk alone, to seek God alone, to find his way along sheep tracks and stream beds, sensing the rightness of the way for himself. He was not afraid to die for his convictions, and opened up a way that is now clear to all. Mountains bring to mind the courage required in walking a spiritual path, a path that each person walks alone, learning to let the silence and stillness speak, free from interference. It is also a reminder that God is found in the natural world when we take time and make effort to seek. Places of organised worship are places for community sharing of thoughts, warmth, caring, healing and praise. The wild places, the solitary places, are where we might well be more likely to experience the truly power-full presence of God.

PRAYER

Lord Jesus, lonely walker on the starlit mountainsides,
the peace and the power you found there, you promised to us.
Lead me on and up, away from the busy noise of everyday life,
to a cave, safe and sheltered, where I can await
the gentle whispering of God.

'This is the sign of the covenant that I make between me and you and every living creature that is with you, for all future generations: I have set my bow in the clouds, and it shall be a sign of the covenant between me and the earth.' — Genesis 9:12 (NRSV)

MIND: Food for thought

WHILE OF COURSE WE NOW KNOW what produces rainbows, and ancient people likewise made the elementary connection between rain and sunshine, they remain a wondrous marvel. It always struck me as a shame that their beauty had to be associated with the gruesome account of the flood, where Yahweh, God of the Old Testament, according to the myth, ordered mass extermination of life because of his anger over human wickedness. I wince when children are told the tale, because straight away they hear the message that God is a terrifying monster, when their first lessons in God should be in learning to trust and love their heavenly Father. I always feel compelled to recount other contemporary myths of the fertile crescent that also describe a flood. One from a country to the north of Israel is very similar but the gods decided to destroy people because they were causing too much noise and pollution in the cities! Fortunately, though, it seems even Yahweh was sorry because the survivors received a promise that never again would there be such retribution for sin. The sign of the promise is the rainbow, a sign that people need never again live in fear of complete annihilation.

BODY: What do you do?

FEEL THAT THE FLOOD STORY is a misused myth, told originally to explain the appearance of rainbows, to recall a real local event and to explain that event in relation to the national relationship with God. It used to be believed that all disasters were deserved; the flood was a disaster, therefore the people who died must have needed punishing (see Job). While people today would not suggest such things about the misfortunes of others, there are times when we interpret personal experiences as punishments. We sometimes look out for punishments when we feel we deserve them, and the habit of linking events to our own behaviour can make us quite morose.

♣ Have you ever felt God was punishing you?

♣ Have you ever been overburdened with guilt and punished yourself?

SPIRIT: Meanings

JESUS BROUGHT US a new way of thinking about God. He taught that God is merciful, like a loving father. Most of all, he brought the message of grace. Grace is the means by which we are accepted by God despite our failings, because God loves us. We can try as hard as we like to live righteously, at the risk of becoming self-righteous, yet we will never be perfect. To be human is to err and, as Jesus found, those who had made the biggest mistakes in their lives were the ones who were most grateful. To feel forgiven allowed them to begin again. Jesus told people that God forgave them, which made the authorities furiously angry, but was what people needed to hear to be healed. We too need to hear that God forgives, we need to learn the value of grace. For the times when we fall down, we need to know that God will help us up, not stamp on us. That is the promise the rainbow gives.

PRAYER

Loving Father God, Loving Lord Jesus,
I have fallen in my weakness and have caused and known great pain.
Now I kneel before you, so small, so sorry,
and I ask for some sign of forgiveness.
As I look up, let me see not anger but kind eyes;
lest I forget your grace, paint a rainbow in my heart.

'You will forget your misery; you will remember it as waters that have passed away.
And your life will be brighter than the noonday ... you will be protected
and take your rest in safety.' — Job 11:16,18 (NRSV)

MIND: Food for thought

IMAGINE A STILL POND, a microcosm of the great sea over which you journey in your life. Every now and then the surface is disturbed by a tiny insect landing, or by a fish beneath the surface. Wherever there is a small impact, a gentle ripple spreads out. When the rain falls, there are so many ripples that they hardly have time to form and spread out before the next begins. The image is one of tranquillity, yet it is easily broken. See yourself taking a large stone and throwing it into the centre of the pond. Now the ripples are much bigger, yet still they radiate in concentric circles to the edges of the pond and break on its bank. But then imagine yourself as a child, not on the bank but standing on a stepping stone, surrounded by water that you suddenly realise is deeper than you thought. You feel a shock of panic, and in you fall. Caught in the pond-weed, slipping on slimy stones and thick mud, you struggle and thrash about. Now, look from above at the effects that child is causing. The peace of the pond has been shattered; the water is churned up into a muddy, treacherous place of fear. The child's splashings make not ripples but turbulent waves that throw everything else into confusion. Now rescue the child, and wait for peace to return.

BODY: What do you do?

I T TAKES CONCENTRATION and understanding to filter all the emotional signals we receive from others. Sometimes other people seem strong and because of their density of thought attract others like a black hole pulling matter in. Unless we recognise their ripples for what they are, as the splashings of a bewildered, struggling soul out of their depth, we too will be pulled in by the force of the waves. They are big waves and carry a lot of psychological clout, but their origin is not calm, controlled strength but the strength which comes through fear. When we make waves, we need to do so with God's purpose in mind.

❖ What instances can you think of where the big waves of others have unsettled you?

❖ When have you caused a big splash that affected others? What was the reason? What were the consequences?

SPIRIT: Meanings

A LL PEOPLE WE ENCOUNTER send out their own ripples of influence and not every disturbance to our circle is unhelpful – at times we need interference to prompt growth. But we must remain vigilant and recognise the causes of disturbance around us. We interact with others, and therefore their ripples, so often that we need to be protected from unwanted and damaging thoughts. Thoughts are spread easily, so it is up to us to be strong-minded enough to hold our own circle dear, to be true to our own feelings and understanding, and to send out not panicky ripples but waves of firm, calm assurance. One way of deepening our sense of God's protective presence encircling us is to use the traditional Celtic caim prayer (as described for example in the Northumbrian Community's *Celtic Daily Prayer Book*). With your index finger, describe a circle around yourself, while uttering a prayer of protection and strength such as the one below. Allow yourself to feel safe at the centre and surrounded by the presence of God.

PRAYER

Father, surround me with a ring of light,
safe within, sure of your might.
Let my circle outwards spread,
firm in hope not weak in dread.

'Now may the Lord of peace himself give you peace at all times in every way.
The Lord be with all of you.' (NIV)
— 2 Thessalonians 3:16

MIND: Food for thought

IMAGINE SNAILS as being the smug version of slugs, having gone one up on hiding under a rock. Their shell makes them an obvious symbol for retreat, the act of removing oneself from an affray, whether a battle or the stresses and strains of everyday life. There are instances in the Gospels where Jesus arranged 'time out' for himself and his disciples, although his intentions were often frustrated. He could only find solitude by depriving himself of sleep. Nevertheless, we all need times when we can withdraw, take stock, review, and rediscover our peace. If we do not take the time, then often 'rests' are forced on us. We become ill, we have an inexplicable accident that means we have to take bed rest for a week, we reach a point where we have to stop. Yet this happens out of self-preservation; we may not need a break if we found life a pleasure and sailed through every moment happily. Life is difficult for most of us, at least some of the time, and we take a lot of strain. We cannot perpetually be in a state of nervous tension like a tightly coiled spring. It is not a sign of fear, but of self-knowledge, to know the right time to go within, to relax into our own shell for a while and remember what peace means.

BODY: What do you do?

WHILE IT IS A VALUABLE LUXURY to be able go on a spiritual retreat, either alone or with like-minded souls, the times we need to be spiritual are the everyday occasions that challenge our whole ethos. We can all be spiritual when we are on retreat, whether living in spiritual community or deliberately isolating ourselves, but it is only of use if it strengthens our sense of the Presence in normal life, with normal people.

❖ Do you only feel at peace when you meditate or pray? Do you feel you need to pray to access your peace? How do you cope with the challenges of everyday life?

❖ Is there a way of bringing peace into your normal approach to life? Can you become a truly peace-full person?

SPIRIT: Meanings

MARCUS AURELIUS, an inspired Roman Emperor writing his *Meditations* in the second century AD, expressed the fact that we can find any number of lonely and/or beautiful places to retreat to. Yet in truth there is no need physically to go anywhere, 'since at any moment you choose you can retire within yourself'. Marcus Aurelius was witness to the peace and tranquillity to be discovered deep within, a knowledge that he shared with Jesus. Both were public figures, one earthly king and one spiritual, who often found it hard to withdraw from the world, yet both knew how to find peace without needing to go anywhere at all. Let us punctuate our thoughts and activities with moments of peace, until we accept fully the gift Christ offers us, of perpetual peace, at all times and in all places.

PRAYER

Lord of Peace,
Join me, curled up tight in my little shell;
curl up with me, and there sing to me in words of gentle wisdom,
until my straining muscles are healed and my restless mind is calmed.
Keep me safe in my shell, then keep me safe as I return to the world, renewed.

'The Lord is my rock, my fortress and my deliverer; my God is my rock in whom I take refuge. He is my shield and the horn of my salvation, my stronghold.' (NIV)

— Psalm 18:2. See also Psalm 9:10, 19:14

MIND: Food for thought

THERE ARE MANY REFERENCES in the Psalms to God as a rock, or the rock. A verse favoured by priests as they stand up to preach is Psalm 19:14, 'May the words of my mouth and the meditation of my heart be pleasing in your sight, O Lord, my rock and my Redeemer.' The rock as a fortress would be a large rocky outcrop, a natural defence. Elsewhere in the Bible we find stones laid down as altars to commemorate sacred events such as the angelic dream of Jacob, or as symbolic witnesses. Our own landscape is punctuated with huge stones, set down thousands of years ago for reasons now obscured by time; whether as temples, huge calendars, shrines to the dead, we can now only speculate. There are those who claim to sense power within these stones, and who believe the stones can in some way connect us to some great 'earth energy'. Such a belief seems to be born from a genuine desire to find a mystical relationship with the world and our roots, although Christians might prefer this 'energy' to be attributed to the God of Love rather than to a finite source.

BODY: What do you do?

WOULD YOU TURN to a stone for strength, or the limitless Power of the universe that brought the stone into being? Whom do you depend on, to the point where you would feel helpless and lost without them? Do you try to make them into rocks? People are not rocks, they move and change like shifting sand.

We need to love our dear ones without placing excessive burdens of expectation on them; for all are free to move with the Spirit and it is not our place to hold them back. It is the word of God, not our human companions, on which we can build the foundations for our dwellings. A house built on sand is not secure and will fall when the storms come. Those known to us who do seem to be able to bear a world on their shoulders deserve our appreciation and love, but we still have no right to take their strength for granted. In releasing our loved ones we find freedom for ourselves too, and the satisfaction that they stay near us through choice, not because they have been trapped.

SPIRIT: Meanings

EVEN STONES CHANGE and break up, even that which seems so solid and sure can be weak; even Peter, called the Rock, denied his master. This is a hard truth to admit to ourselves, as it speaks of loneliness and separation, of distance and of poverty of communication with even those we love most. Everything, perhaps everyone, is ultimately capable of letting us down, not necessarily through any fault, but by the nature of mortality and physical vulnerability. But Spirit is infinite, unbound by the physical laws of decay and weakness. The Spirit is reliable; it is constant and ever-present in all, without fail. In turning to God for help we find our needs are met in unexpected ways and through unexpected people. We become less bound to individuals and more confident that the Spirit will never leave us alone. Stone is thus a symbol of trust in God, the source of true power and strength, and a sobering reminder that all that is finite shifts and changes over time.

PRAYER

Father, my rock, all in this world shifts like the sands.
You alone are constant.
All in this world one day breathes its last breath.
Your power alone lives on.
I would seek out a cave as my dwelling,
in you would I make my refuge, my Father, my rock.

'The sun shall no longer be your light by day, nor for brightness shall the moon give light to you by night; but the Lord will be your everlasting light, and your God will be your glory.' — Isaiah 60:19 (NRSV)

MIND: Food for thought

THE SUN HAS BEEN A SYMBOL of God since ancient times. As our source of light and life the sun gives hope, warmth and gladness, and fills us with awe. Various cultures have worshipped the sun in its own right, which provides us with a warning against worshipping any thing. The sun has no awareness, it is not living. It cannot reciprocate our attentions in any way . Anything that we single out to be our focus of worship, whether it be money, machines or power, will not bend to us, will not speak to our spirit; it will simply become an obsession. We might believe the same about God, yet the inspired lives of many believers attest otherwise. Like the sun, God is incorruptible and shines on, despite our turning to and away from the light in the course of our journeying. Sunshine is for all; there is no bar on receiving blessings unless we choose to shut ourselves away. Not a person, not a life-form but an energy, God is radiance, dynamic and pure. God is the shining source of Love, Joy, Peace, every attribute that gladdens our hearts and brings freedom to our souls. There is no place in God for impurity. All that is not of God will burn up like chaff before it even approaches; all malice and hatred will be reduced to nothing.

BODY: What do you do?

THE CHALLENGE OF THE SUN as a symbol is to learn to love the thought of God and to want the presence of God more than anything, for the presence of God is Love.

❖ As a child, how did you think of God? In what ways has your thinking moved on since then? Have you stopped thinking? Have you started rejecting?

❖ Do you believe in God? How would you describe this entity that you either dismiss or accept? Could you alter your belief? Jesus said we must love God wholeheartedly. How can we until we have a definite impression of God's love for us?

❖ Have you ever asked God for evidence, then explained away any response as a fluke?

❖ Do you worship any thing? Do you have an ambition in life? Do you have an obsession that occupies your mind?

SPIRIT: Meanings

OUR MISDIRECTED WORSHIP continues, like a moth drawn to a deadly flame, until we too reach our wilderness fire, the point in our lives where we realise we have been misguided. The drives to achieve luxury, wealth and prestige eventually burn out and we realise it is more important to have genuine love, wisdom and peace of mind, for these are the only lasting qualities. It can be a shock to realise that the goal we have always set ourselves means nothing, or that our ambition serves only the illusion of our self-importance. Our true goals need to focus on the qualities of Godliness, on the exploration of wisdom, of beauty, of creativity, of understanding of the natural world, of the depths of love and the heights of spiritual peace. In aiming to find God we cannot fail, for God is closer to us than sunbeams. In truth, God has already found us, for all are included in the warmth.

PRAYER

God of Light, help me to understand your nature,
that I may speak of you in wisdom, not in foolishness.
Let me sense your presence as I might sense sunlight warming my skin,
let me shine with the qualities that are your essence,
let me know you, that I may love you.

'When they bring you before the synagogues, the rulers and the authorities, do not worry about how you are to defend yourselves or what you are to say; for the Holy Spirit will teach you at that very hour what to say.' — Luke 12:11–12 (NRSV)

MIND: Food for thought

GOD IS THE GREAT VOICE, God is the great song; in the creation myth of Genesis, God's breath was over the waters and he uttered sound to create. All things were made as God expressed his volition: 'Let there be ...' I have always treasured the account in the C.S. Lewis Narnia tale, *The Magician's Nephew*, where Aslan the lion brings all life into being through song. From our own experience, there is much in the wisdom literature of the Bible warning us against hasty speech and words uttered in anger, for words have so much power. Jesus too advised caution, for our words come from our hearts and can reveal either goodness or poison. But the quotation above has a specific context. It was a promise for the early church as it struggled with persecution and demands to justify confidence in Jesus as God's Messiah. It is a special message addressing a real anxiety. People were being imprisoned and tortured simply for their beliefs and they were afraid. What could they say? What should they say? We are often not aware that we are being put in the dock for our faith, yet whenever we dare to speak with the voice of truth, justice and peace then we are standing for Jesus. It is at these times, when our sense of what is right comes under scrutiny, that we need to trust the Spirit of Truth to speak in us, not the spirit of timidity and indecision, for whatever we say has repercussions.

BODY: What do you do?

❖ When you are put to the test, do you speak out of fear, desperate to defend yourself, or do you let a higher truth filter through?

❖ When defending yourself means lying or covering up the facts, what do you do?

❖ When you could heal or wreck a situation by your choice of words, how do you decide what to say?

❖ Why did Jesus refrain from defending himself at his trial? Are we required to follow this difficult example, or does the quotation above give us hope that we will be helped?

❖ Which is more important: to speak the truth, or to speak words of peace? Is this an unreasonable question?

SPIRIT: Meanings

T O COMMUNICATE WITH GOD, maybe we should brush up on our own harmonies. Communication with God is about finding harmony with God, it is not just about repeating the right words or going to church. If we are in discord with God then everything jars, everything makes us wince and hunch up, trying to block out the sound. We need to discover for ourselves the resonant frequencies that God utters. Maybe they are so deep we usually mistake them for rumbles of thunder, or so high they are beyond our range. But bring any note down or up a few octaves and there it is, ready for us to sing. So what frequency is love? What frequency is peace? These attributes belong together as rich, soothing chords. Hate and fear are the notes that do not belong in the chord at all; it is these that we need to be able to locate and silence.

PRAYER

Spirit of Truth, sometimes I don't even realise I should be speaking out until it is too late.
Make me bold enough to say the words you give me;
make me wise enough to mull over my own words well, before I dare to let them loose.
Make me perceptive enough to know the difference.

*'He split rocks open in the wilderness, and gave them drink abundantly
as from the deep. He made streams come out of the rock, and caused waters
to flow down like rivers.'* — Psalm 78:15–16 (NRSV)

MIND: Food for thought

I N THE AIR, IN THE GROUND, falling and rising, running as a stream, a
river, an ocean, within each living thing, sustaining life, uniting the Earth,
water, like the presence of the Spirit, is everywhere. Water on Earth is all-
powerful: moving and still, internal and external, life-giving and life-taking.
Like the power of Spirit, it is at once beautiful, powerful, awesome, gentle,
never-ending and, like the oceans, unfathomable. Water demonstrates,
through physical connection of all life, the truth of spiritual unity. In watching a river flow we are reminded too of our own journey, back to the infinite
Ocean of Love. While we may feel that we travel alone, it is the Spirit within
us that wills for union and urges us on. But just as water is essentially water
wherever it is and in whichever state, so do we hold the essence of that which
we are seeking to become. We each have intrinsic spiritual worth which means
that in one sense, at the depth of our being, we have already arrived: the rain-
drop holds the essence of both the clouds and the sea. Just as water moves
through its huge cycle, so too do we journey through our spiritual spiral. We
travel through many cycles of our own in our quest for wisdom and depth,
but we eventually return to the point at which we started: the Ocean of
Peaceful Love.

BODY: What do you do?

SEA WATER INVITES US to go deeper: deeper into the blue-green other-world and deeper into ourselves, to find the meaning, the peace, the comfort, which we can only find by diving beneath the surface. In finding this incredible depth within ourselves, we start to see disturbances as somehow removed from the inner calm that we possess. This inner calm is our true centre, our beginning point, where we communicate constantly with the Spirit of Love. This calm is the Great Calm that dispels all fear. Here we realise that we can go deep, away from the surface-level turbulence around us. We can dive down to our own pool of tranquillity and become one with all who do the same.

♣ There is such a wealth of symbolism in the many forms water takes. You might use each aspect of the water cycle, including the presence of water within living organisms, in your meditations. Trace references to water in the Bible, perhaps starting with John 4:13–15, where Jesus speaks of 'a spring of water gushing up to eternal life'.

SPIRit: Meanings

WHILE OUR OWN QUESTS for enlightenment seem to spiral on for ever, it is a comfort to know that our searching is shared and that another has entered before us into the timeless dimension of Peace, to be in some way with us now. For the spirit of the one who reaches the Heart of God becomes one with God, just as rivers run into the ocean. We already have the Spirit within us, and Spirit is Spirit wherever it is. We may think of ourselves as vessels of the Spirit, yet I prefer to think of caves. We are like a rain-soaked hillside over which water flows, gradually wearing a channel. In time, the channel deepens, penetrating even through rock until the water finds a way underground. It carves out an incredible passageway within us, through which it can cascade, always shaping and wearing away the resisting rock. To explore an underground watercourse is to see the sheer power of water. We too are shaped inside until we have not a little stream but a rushing torrent of Spirit deep within.

PRAYER

Father of the Ocean, you never leave us, but are at once within the very cells of our bodies and running over our skin like rain. Let me not resist the channel you make in me; I would be like a great cavern filled with the roaring, rushing energy of your Spirit.

'Now in Jerusalem by the Sheep Gate there is a pool, called in Hebrew Bethezda …
One man was there who had been ill for thirty-eight years.
When Jesus saw him lying there and knew that he had been there a long time,
he said to him, "Do you want to be made well?"' – John 5:1–9 (NRSV)

MIND: Food for thought

NATURAL SPRINGS have always been seen as precious, for obvious reasons. But as well as providing water, they seem in many cases to have been associated with miraculous events such as healings. Many shrines can be found in the countryside of the British Isles, and local history books frequently explain that although a spring now bears a saint's name, it was previously associated with nature spirits or local deities. There is rarely much more that scholars can tell us about ancient practices, unless artifacts have been found in the bed, whereupon the suggestion is made of 'votive offerings'! This situation reflects the great difficulty people in the British Isles experience in attempting to discover their roots. We are always in danger of idealising, of fantasising, and projecting our own assumptions onto the beliefs of long ago, based on objects that we find. There is a real longing to reconnect with the old ways, hence the reconstruction of druidism using 19th-century theories, and the 'renewal' of paganism and Wicca. None of these cults really know what happened in the past. The traditions they lay claim to are not rooted in ancient and verifiable documents, for there are none; nor are there reliable oral traditions dating back more than a few hundred years. There are however some rather gruesome remains which indicate that the old religions were certainly not all peace and light! Rather than trying to reinvent the past as a way of lending authority to current beliefs and practices, perhaps it is more appropriate to use genuine authorities, for which we do have information, to guide our thinking in the present.

BODY: What do you do?

THE CONCISE OXFORD DICTIONARY defines a miracle as 'an extra-ordinary event attributed to some supernatural agency'. Have you ever experienced anything that might fit this definition, or are you cynical about the possibility?

❖ How do you respond to the accounts of healings by Jesus? Do you believe them? Do you seek to rationalise them? Is there a consistent pattern running through them all? Does it make you feel angry that people in Jesus's day experienced miracles, yet you, or your loved ones today, are struggling with sickness? Is this an issue you bring before God, or is it one that makes you feel distant from God?

❖ Does it matter that people still venerate natural features such as springs and trees? Does it matter that people claim to be following in ancient traditions that are often based on conjecture?

SPIRIT: Meanings

THE QUOTATION above comes from an account describing how people believed an angel came to stir the waters of the pool, and that the first person to enter the water would be healed. The description is so vivid, it must come from a person who was well acquainted with that site in Jerusalem. So here we have the kind of evidence that earth-mystics in Britain would dearly love to have, to give them 'authority' for their rituals. Yet, there is no evidence that Jesus believed in the efficacy of the spring; he did not offer to lift the man into the water, he merely ascertained whether the man really did want healing, and gave him the instruction to get up. We can have faith in many things, some of which amount to superstition, some which arise from our need for meaning, yet Jesus had faith in only one thing: God. He worked healings through an innate understanding of the will and the active power of God. This is where we too need to look if we are hoping for a miracle.

PRAYER

Lord, let me put my faith in you, not in empty rituals or places.
May I always be open to the possibility of miracles, but in asking let me not lose heart,
for your will is beyond me.

*'I remember the devotion of your youth, how as a bride you loved me
and followed me through the desert, through a land not sown.'* (NIV)
— Jeremiah 2:2,6. See also Isaiah 40:3, Matthew 3:3, Matt 4:1

MIND: Food for thought

THE HEBREWS WANDERED IN THE WILDERNESS; John the Baptist drew crowds there to hear his message; Jesus was compelled by the Spirit to go to the desert after his baptism. The wilderness, the wildness, is a place beyond the refuge of civilisation. It is the domain of wild creatures, having ceased to be our natural habitat long ago. At first sight it is a place of arid desolation, of hopeless wandering, endless and pitiless. Here we are brought to our knees, face to face with our own loneliness, our vulnerability and dependence on each other. Here we sink down low, reeling from blows that hit hard where we are softest. This is the place where we fall after our pride finally trips us up. This is the place where all that we thought we knew is turned round. This is the place where all the challenges we dared to utter towards the power of God, all the arguments we used to try to persuade God to see things our way, are shown in their true and ridiculous light. We are suddenly crushed by our own smallness. This is the place where we have to face the truth; and it can hurt. But it is also the place where people have found and followed God.

BODY: What do you do?

SOME OF US STUMBLE into our wilderness unawares. Some visit once and never return; some seem to get lost and lose hope of anything different, wallowing in their own misery and dragging others in with them. Only those already close to the Truth go knowingly and willingly, prepared to face their lowest depths to find the highest peace. Those who go to the wilderness meet the emptiness and the wholeness of themselves, their weakness and then, sometimes, their wisdom.

❖ Which of the above applies to you now?

❖ At the lowest points in your life, what changed for you? How did you pull through, or are you still waiting for rescue?

❖ In your wilderness, what is the greatest emotion? Fear? Guilt? Loss? Anger? Self-pity? Are these feelings you can ask for help with?

SPIRIT: Meanings

GOD REQUIRES OUR ALL. Everything that stands between us and God is what we have to lose. The desert is the place where we feel that loss. Jesus himself went into the wilderness to meet temptation, and emerged empowered, with integrity intact. He gave his all to become a homeless wanderer, driven by an urgent message of acceptance for society's rejects and the immanence of God's power. But Jesus was a man who went knowingly into the wilderness. He had nothing more to lose and could walk unafraid. For us the wilderness is a terrible place at first because it is the home of our self-centredness and self-importance. Once we have been stripped bare and forced to accept our own emptiness, then, and only then, can we be filled by that deeper peace which the world cannot give. Only then do we begin to appreciate the emptiness for what it really is.

PRAYER

Lord Jesus,
You did not shy from the wilderness
but emerged victorious.
In my own struggles, watch over me
for I am weak but you are strong.

HUMAN-MADE OBJECTS

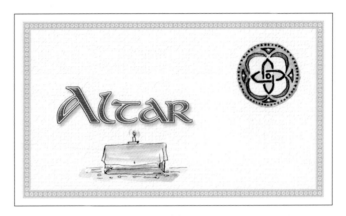

'Therefore, if you are offering your gift at the altar and there remember that your brother has something against you, leave your gift there in front of the altar. First go and be reconciled to your brother; then come and offer your gift.' — Matthew 5:23–24 (NIV)

MIND: Food for thought

AN ALTAR is a place where we deliberately make an offering to God. In literal terms it is normally a stone or wooden table, sometimes decorated, often bearing a candle or some other symbol of spiritual presence. In ancient times, an altar was used to demonstrate thanks, guilt, commitment, or anything that it seemed right to take out of human hands and place in the power of the Great Spirit. In the world of the Old Testament, altars were for sacrifice, the solemn business of offering up life itself. They were bound up with contemporary beliefs in gods – or God – who required death for sins (see ALDER). The word 'sacrifice' means to set apart as sacred or holy. It involves handing over small-scale human power to the one great spiritual power. In Christian thinking, the altar has taken on a new significance. As well as being a point at which offerings are made, it is also a place of communion, of sharing bread and wine, and giving thanks. Rather than a place of death, it is a place of life, a place to meet the God of Merciful Love.

BODY: What do you do?

IF WE THROW PETALS IN THE SEA to mark our entrusting to God, or play a melody into the wind for God to hear our sadness; if we set down a rock in a place where we met deep love or witnessed a beautiful sight; if we place a feather on the bookshelf to remind us of our spiritual freedom, these are altars. They are points created to demonstrate communication with God, times of giving thanks, sharing feeling, seeking solace, letting go, needing help.

❖ What altars can you set up? They need not be obvious to anyone but you!

❖ What would you offer to God in thanks? What guilt do you need to let go of?

❖ How do you interpret the idea of being a 'living sacrifice'?

❖ How do you feel about surrendering everything to God? Relieved, or worried?

SPIRIT: Meanings

TO MEET AT THE ALTAR and share bread and wine is to raise 'fruit of the earth and work of human hands' to the level of the sacred; for these not only represent but in some sense are the body and blood of Christ. What claim is this? That Christ's body is the fruit of the soil combined with our labour, and as the earth is broken for our benefit, so was the body of Christ.

Thus, the altar has become a point at which we can come to share the truth that Christ is in the living world around us, which we are responsible for and which we depend on for nourishment. The eating of bread and drinking of wine demonstrates the oneness not only of the gathered community, but of all in which Christ dwells. From another perspective, the altar reminds us of the act of surrender, not to oppressors but to God, our liberator. We might learn something from Islam here: the very word Islam means 'submission to God'.

PRAYER

All that I am, all that I have,
all whom I love and struggle to love,
every weight that I bear and all that I think,
all that I do, every word and creation of mine,
I place in your hands, Lord.
All that I need,
I receive back from you.

'He made my mouth like a sharp sword, in the shadow of his hand he hid me;
he made me a polished arrow, in his quiver he hid me away ...' (NRSV)
— Isaiah 49:2

MIND: Food for thought

T HE QUOTATION ABOVE is interesting as it takes the symbols of arrows, targets and achievable goals so loved by business consultants and adds a new dimension. Huge pressure is put on employees, businesses and even children at school to meet target after target in a relentless push for progress. We live in a very achievement-orientated culture, where we are not just encouraged to set ourselves projects for self-motivation, we become part of a machine that has to increase productivity and improve results. We are allowed to believe, by the powers that be, that we have ownership of these targets, but really they are part of a much bigger picture. We are being driven to bring improvements to our company, school or society, and in the process we are cajoled into feeling good about it. But true goals need to be weighed more carefully. They are not to do with productivity and exam results; they are to do with personal self-development and fulfilment. In working life it can become difficult to see the wood for the trees; there are so many targets, yet few of them have intrinsic worth unless they contribute to our spiritual growth. The writer of Isaiah 49 takes the target as the restoration of Israel, but the arrow is not some abstract concept; it is God's own servant, in this case the faithful remnant of the children of Israel. The person is not the archer, but the arrow. If God is the archer, the arrow will follow a true course.

BODY: What do you do?

D O YOU SEE THE BIBLE as a big 'This Way' sign through life? If yes, what do you do when you encounter contradictory messages from the text? If no, do you take some other scriptural text as your basic pointer, or are you just finding your own way? If you are just finding your own way, what is it about the scriptures you have encountered that you mistrust so much and why? Do you believe you would be required to accept them lock, stock and barrel? Do you accept that there may be some shred of wisdom that would help guide you? If yes, then read until you find it. If no, then write the wisdom you wish you could read and see how it stands up!

✤ How do you respond to the idea of going home as your main target in life?

✤ If God is the archer, does it mean that life is predetermined?

SPIRIT:Meanings

T HE BOW AND ARROW has such a long history it is used as a symbol almost without thinking. Yet we can escape from the linear nature of arrow flight, we can change the imagery a little to be true to the Celtic fondness for spirals and circles. Take the above quotation and substitute a boomerang for the arrow. The biblical people couldn't do this because they were not aware of Australia, but we can. Now we have God, who throws out a projectile, with a clear 'mission', yet instead of its landing some great distance away, it comes back. What are our lives but a great round-trip to return to our home ? Physically, we come from (star) dust and return to (star) dust; spiritually we are of eternal Spirit and our spirit must be drawn back into oneness. Our journey through life has an aim: to do the will of the thrower and then to go home.

PRAYER

My strong-armed Father,
my source and my destination,
my power and my resting place,
you trusted me to be borne on the air,
you let me free on my journey through life;
even though I forget your will and miss your mark,
still, welcome me home, for I am yours.

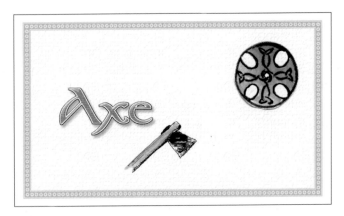

'… male and female he created them. God blessed them and said to them,
"Be fruitful and increase in number; fill the earth and subdue it." … God saw all that
he had made, and it was very good.' — Genesis 1:27–28 & 31 (NIV)

MIND: Food for thought

THE AXE represents our own destructive power and potential. The way we each wield our axe is the way we have chosen to interpret the words of Genesis 1:28 where man and woman are given responsibility for the living world. Do we believe in the words 'dominate' and 'subjugate' or do we wince when we read particular translations and wish for the presence of a wise Hebrew scholar? The reckless progress of our society into industrialisation, mercilessly dragging the whole world in our wake in their awakened desire for material betterment, is testimony to the license that was found historically in that single verse. The axe is a tool of violence. It cannot be used without determination and the strength of the whole body behind it. Its power can be horribly misused, to maim and kill and decimate. It is thus a symbol of all deliberately destructive acts, both on a physical level and on a mental level. The axe can have a more benign meaning, however. An axe in safe hands represents human use of power to sustain the interrelatedness of life so that all might benefit, all might be nurtured, supported and appreciated, or simply left in peace. Thus, the axe can mean domination and subjugation, but we are now collectively waking to the realisation that this approach will in effect scuttle our own ship. The axe can also mean recognising responsibility and the ability to create order, the human capacity to think beyond our small selves to the wider picture of the whole Earth, and the generations that will follow us.

BODY: What do you do?

LOOK WITH HONESTY at your every action. On balance, do you do more to care for the earth or to harm it? Do you drive when you could walk? When you could put on a jumper do you turn up the heaters? Do you buy battery farm eggs when you could buy free-range ones? I have had to plead guilty on several counts at some time or other. What about you?

❖ It has been said that evil is what happens when good people do nothing. How do you respond to this statement in the context of caring for the earth?

❖ Do you feel that the people who represent you in parliament and your spiritual group reflect your concerns for the environment and act appropriately? If not, would you consider addressing this discrepancy?

SPIRIT: Meanings

THE CONFIDENCE WE NEED to wield our axes rightly lies not our own self-centred power but the Power of the Greatest Good, the active principle of God, the traditional energy of the angelic host, the power of compassion and love for all life. With this strength in our arms we can begin to imagine ourselves as responsible caretakers of the Earth, trustees of the most precious gift to our descendants. The symbol of the axe does not represent a situation where we can sit back and wait for God to create a dreamy idyll complete with lions lying down with lambs. It is a sharp reminder that we must involve ourselves with the loving management of Earth, because if we do not we will witness destruction unspeakable in its sadness and senselessness. The charge of responsibility was put on our shoulders, as our intelligence and sense of morality set us apart from other animals. We need to use those gifts for the good of the whole of creation.

PRAYER

Lord, your world is so beautiful.
Teach us to be careful guardians of life,
teach us to act wisely for the good of all.

'Do not judge, so that you may not be judged. For with the judgement you make you will be judged, and the measure you give will be the measure you get.' (NRSV)
— Matthew 7:1–2

MIND: Food for thought

MEASUREMENTS ARE CALCULATED using a standard weight on a balance. We weigh each other up in an agreed way using a clearly defined set of moral guidelines for the sake of maintaining law and order; and, on a personal basis, using our own gut reactions. Where we feel there is a discrepancy between the 'standard unit' of society's judgement and our own sense of right and wrong, then conflict arises, and when we disagree with our neighbour over arbitrary or subjective instances of right and wrong, there is animosity. We have strongly held opinions, sometimes based on experience, and sometimes based on lack of it. Jesus pointed out that the one who has sinned most is likely to be the most forgiving; our own error often gives us greater compassion and generosity of spirit for those who have also made mistakes. Tolerance, forgiveness and mutual understanding are more worthy attributes than self-righteousness and judgementalism. Yet the concept of balance is important. We find as we go through life that there are fewer absolutes than we thought, and conversely there are more grey areas. We find ourselves debating not so much about good/bad, black/white but about where there is a point of reconciliation. It is the pivot on the see-saw that becomes interesting, rather than the oscillations of the two ends.

BODY: What do you do?

I ALWAYS REMEMBER a conversation with a friend, where we were discussing confession. She said she didn't see any need to go to confession because she hadn't done anything wrong. This irritated me for some time because I could see several points she might not be so proud of. Years later, it occurred to me that really I should have been less concerned with her apparent self-righteousness and more concerned with my own haste in judging my friend. We need to beware of falling into the role of Job's friends, who tried to tell him what his problem was, although they really had no idea.

❧ What is your response to the quotation from 1 Samuel 16:7, where God advises Samuel to choose David as king? 'For the Lord does not see as mortals see; they look on the outward appearance, but the Lord looks on the heart.'

SPIRIT: Meanings

THE TRIANGULAR RELATIONSHIP between good, bad and compromise only goes so far. There is great attraction in the oriental philosophy of the balance of opposites, which often might well describe the earthly state. Yet we must be careful of suggesting that the ultimate reality is also a balance of opposites, that there is a dualism between forces of good and evil. While this idea might be exciting in film scripts, God is not at the mercy of fiction writers and transcends that which is evil. There is no place in God for anything but perfect good. God is not the weight on the balance; God is not the pivot, the middle ground of compromise; God is not the object to be weighed, for there is nothing that can counterbalance God. God is the heart that knows there will always be an imbalance between divine goodness and human weakness, and adds blessings until the weakness is compensated for by love. With God, there is only love.

PRAYER

Loving Father, counterbalance my fear with your love,
my confusion with the certainty of your strength.
When you weigh my many sins, may you also find enough love to tip the scales.
When I prepare to put others on the balance, remind me of
the standard of measure you use.
Let me look only at hearts and be ready to give my own love, when it is needed.

*'A furious squall came up, and the waves broke over the boat,
so that it was nearly swamped.'* (NIV)
— Mark 4:37. See also: Matthew 8:24, 14:28, Mark 6:51, Luke 8:22

MIND: Food for thought

IF WE CONSTRUCT AND SAIL OUR CRAFT with awareness of the environment and sensitivity to the moods of the winds and waves we can hope, after a lifetime of experience, to be at one with the elements. Without this wisdom we remain at the mercy of every gust. Boats had great significance in the culture of the New Testament, whether for fishing on the Sea of Galilee or travelling across the Mediterranean. Jesus was entirely familiar with sailing and the sea, and used boats as we might use taxis. In the story from which the above quotation is taken, where Jesus stills the storm, we can read 'mental turmoil' for 'storm', and 'pray to' for 'wake', thus discovering a clear message about the power of prayer in supporting our passage through life's troubles. The same story reminds us however that there is an element of mortal risk in taking to the seas. I remember, as a girl, looking out one night over a busy Cornish harbour. I was fascinated by the play of lights on the water below, but I was even more poetically drawn to the mysterious darkness of the sea beyond. That same night a little motor boat with local lads but inadequate life-jackets, engine power and knowledge of the rocks and currents, set out into the darkness, looking for adventure. The next morning the whole village was searching for bodies. It is easy to be wise after the event, but such a tragedy reminds us not only to respect natural forces, but also to avoid romanticising that which can overwhelm us.

BODY: What do you do?

WHEN YOUR 'BOAT' CAPSIZES, do you blame God or do you look to your own sailing skills? Do you ever take risks in the name of religious belief? Wherein lies your confidence?

❖ Do you rely on others to get you through life, or do you accept responsibility for your own craft?

❖ Would you be surprised to find Jesus curled up asleep in your boat? While we are each sailing our own craft through life, born alone and dying alone, there is a sense in which we are not alone, for the presence of Christ, true man of Galilee, is with every sailor, ready to still our storms and take away our fears. He waits, at peace, until we ask for his intervention.

❖ Would you be happy about letting Christ sail your boat?

SPIRIT: Meanings

THE BOAT REPRESENTS the effort of our journey through life. The water under the boat represents God's presence, which supports us. The wind in the sails is the energy of the Spirit. Even the smallest changes in wind direction need to be acted upon to avoid trouble, but a skilled sailor can also make quite steady progress on barely a breath. Likewise we can let the Spirit be the energy in our lives. If we are sensitive enough, maybe it will even chart our route for us. Considering our faith in the invisible forces that keep aeroplanes up, it should not trouble us that the Holy Spirit is invisible; like the wind in the sails and on the surface of the water, we can see its effects well enough. The alternative is to rely on our own little power, which seems to me like being given a choice between a yacht and a rowing boat. Thus, we have to decide whether to struggle on alone, afraid of the waves and the wind, unsure even of our direction, let alone our ability; or whether to ask for Christ to wake up and do it his way.

PRAYER

Christ who stills storms, wake up within me and still the storms of my life.
Teach me to understand the signs of the Spirit's breath.
Christ who walks on the waters, come out to me, alone in my little boat.

'Give us today our daily bread. Forgive us our debts,
as we also have forgiven our debtors.' (NIV)
— Matthew 6:11–12

MIND: Food for thought

THERE IS HARDLY A BOOK in the Bible that does not mention bread at least once. In its various forms it was the staple diet of Bible times and the word could be used to mean all or any food. The quotation above, from the Lord's prayer, can be taken as a request to meet the essentials of life, and echoes the words of the Sermon on the Mount, 'Therefore I tell you, do not worry about your life, what you will eat or what you will drink, or about your body, what you will wear. Is not life more than food, and the body more than clothing? ...' (Matthew 6:25) This in turn reflects the response Jesus is recorded as giving to the devil during his temptation: 'It is written that one does not live by bread alone but by every word that comes from the mouth of God.' (Matthew 4:4, quoting from Deuteronomy 8:3) We often find in the Gospels that Jesus's disciples are preoccupied with where their next meal will come from, and are taken aback by Jesus's attitude. In John 4:31, for example, they urge him to eat but he tells them that his food is to do the will of the One who sent him. In John 6, his disciples mention the gift of manna, given to the Israelites wandering in the wilderness. They are hoping to elicit a miracle from Jesus. Jesus however replies that he is the bread from heaven, he is the bread of life. This is affirmed during the Last Supper, where broken bread became the lasting reminder of Jesus's death.

BODY: What do you do?

SOMETIMES WE NEED TO REFLECT on what we consider our needs to be. Our basic human needs for survival are quite simple: adequate food and water, shelter, clothing, sleep. We know we also have emotional needs: to feel safe, loved and understood. Then we have our individual needs: the healing of a sickness, the means to travel, the means to communicate over distance with a loved one. But it is easy to let wants creep into the needs list. Modern consumerism reflects demand; we know when we are being greedy.

❖ What do you count as 'daily bread'?

❖ What extra abundance comes to you that you need to give thanks for?

❖ How far do you go in meeting the needs of others?

SPIRIT: Meanings

WE, LIKE THE ISRAELITES wandering in the wilderness, are very conscious of our bodily needs, but Jesus asks us, like the same Israelites, to trust that God who sent them manna will also help us. We are asked to trust that God will provide, thus giving us the freedom to fix our mind on our spiritual needs. If we ask we will be answered, if we seek we will find and if we knock the door will be opened, for God knows what we need even before we ask. 'Do not worry saying "What shall we eat," or "What shall we drink ..." Strive first for the kingdom of God and his righteousness, and all these things will be given to you as well.' (Matthew 6:33) Thus, we must put one need above all others, and that is the need to discover the kingdom of God for ourselves, because in so doing we find that all our other needs are met.

PRAYER

Loving Father, you know what I need before I ask;
help me to see for myself what I truly need.

'The head of that statue was of fine gold, its chest and arms of silver, its middle and thighs of bronze, its legs of iron and its feet partly of iron and partly of clay ...' (NRSV)
— Daniel 2:31–35

MIND: Food for thought

ARTIFACTS FROM OUR HISTORY are rich in carvings and images of figures which seem to represent gods or goddesses. Whether these objects themselves were felt to have power or whether they had a symbolic role is impossible to know. There has been a tendency in many cultures to express divinity through an object, an attempt which must surely always fall short of the Truth itself, due to the limitations of materials and our own understanding. The contemporary issue is perhaps less to do with the worship of graven idols, however, and more to do with the adulation of human idols. We live in a world where some have ascended to giddy heights of fame: our stars are richer, more beautiful, more powerful than ever before. But the trouble is, despite all this, they are also as human as they have ever been. Public interest puts such people on pedestals for all to see and admire, but the moment one of these heroes shows some sign of human error and weakness, the same public interest brings them crashing down. It is as though, like in Nebuchadnezzar's dream about the wonderful god-statue, their feet are made of crumbling clay (Daniel 2:31). Even Jesus wished to avoid being set on a pedestal: when somebody addressed him as 'good Teacher', he retorted, 'Why do you call me good? Nobody is good but God alone.' (Mark 10:17–18)

BODY: What do you do?

ON A DAY TO DAY BASIS, we need to consider which people we place on pedestals, whether politicians, colleagues, musicians or ministers of religion. Whom do we place in a position of elevation above 'mere mortals' because we feel they are wiser, nobler, braver or more intelligent than everyone else? In creating our own idols, we put others in a position from which it is very difficult to climb down without an undignified fall, and we also open ourselves to disillusionment.

❖ Who have you placed on a pedestal?

❖ Have you ever been on a pedestal yourself? How did you get down? Or are you still there? Take care!

❖ What is your response to Jesus's retort, 'Why do you call me good?'

SPIRIT: Meanings

WHILE WE SHOULD make a point of looking for qualities, we should also accept the intrinsic human nature common to all. In King Nebuchadnezzar's dream, he was himself the head of gold, but the foundation of the statue was brittle clay. It could not support the huge weight pressing down on it and was bound to collapse. We too are like clay, as Job realised: 'Remember that you moulded me like clay. Will you now turn me to dust again?' (Job 10:9) Job was another example of a great and even righteous man brought low. The belief at the time was that misfortune was always deserved, and thus Job suffered not only illness and terrible loss, but also the indignity of ridicule. We do not know the truth behind peoples' lives, however much the media feeds us. Our place is to show compassion and generosity of heart to all, regardless of status, popularity or wealth. True treasure, after all, is in the heart.

PRAYER

*Father, you see your children as equal
and love us all.
Help me to see greatness in spiritual terms
and to remember that only you are perfect.*

'... *and everyone who sought the Lord would go out*
to the tent of meeting ...' (NRSV)
— Exodus 33:7–11

MIND: Food for thought

TENTS FEATURE prominently in the Bible. The nomadic Hebrews fleeing from Egypt spent many years living like the Bedouin, under skin and felt shelters. They knew what it was like to wander with no sense of permanence or belonging, yet they felt they were being led to a home where they could settle. The tale of the Exodus is that of transition from nomad to farmer, from dependence on sheep and goats to dependence on corn, olives and vines. As a symbol of God's presence amongst them as they journeyed, they constructed the tabernacle, a glorious tent in which to house the ark of the covenant. In this tent the leaders could consult the will of God by casting sacred stones, the Urim and Thummim, kept in a pouch in the priestly garments. It was a most sacred place, yet it could be moved, for God was not tied to one place, He was wherever they were, leading them in a pillar of fire. Jesus went a step further in his demonstration of impermanence; he didn't even have a tent as far as we can see, but relied on the hospitality of friends during his journeys. But unlike the ancient Hebrews, Jesus did not have a portable shrine and a set of stones. Jesus was the shrine, and he knew the mind of God without needing to consult anybody or anything. But, like the Hebrews, he too was in a limbo-state; he was on his way to a home better than any literal land flowing with milk and honey. Listening to the words of Afro-American spiritual songs, we often hear reference to that other place, that 'home in gloryland', that was such an important hope to a displaced and uprooted people. Tents thus represent the transience of life, and the hope of heaven, but at the same time the experience of God here and now, wherever we are.

BODY: What do you do?

HAVE YOU EVER EMPLOYED a system of divination to determine the will of God? It is a very ancient art, found in many cultures, from the *I Ching* of China, to the runes of the Norse people, to the Tarot of the Romanies. Divination was used in court to determine matters of state, like the Urim and Thummim (Shall we go to war with the Philistines, yes or no? 1 Samuel 28:6, 2 Samuel 5:17–25), as much as in personal life. Why do you feel people believe in such practices? Do you think they ever work? Might God use stones and cards and scratches on shells to communicate? Does it depend on the wisdom of the interpretation? Might they mislead? Is it dangerous? Does it frighten, fascinate or repel you? Is it superfluous, given the guidance of Jesus and the Holy Spirit, through prayer?

How do you imagine your 'promised land'?

SPIRIT: Meanings

WE CAN SEE OURSELVES in the same state of journeying as the ancient Hebrews, uncomfortable, sometimes ungrateful and obstinate, sometimes fearful, but with the firm leadership of Moses and the pillar of fire to follow. Moses might represent the law, the importance of obedience to a sense of morality, while the fire might represent the inspirational power of Spirit, always beyond us, but always there. But as we journey, we have the influence of Jesus. He is our Urim and Thummim, our sacred stone; he is our point of communication, the reason why we can begin to understand God's will for each decision we make. Those stones were the only form of divination accepted by the writers of the Old Testament (although they were never described as such), the possession of which allowed David to call himself a Priest King. But we have Jesus to show us the way as we journey, the greatest Priest King of all, who had no need for casting stones for guidance. Let us follow him.

PRAYER

Lord, I don't need anything but an open heart and mind to realise your will. Let me trust that you hear me when I pray, and that you answer me in any way I am able to hear. Let me know your presence as I journey; give me wisdom to discriminate between those who communicate your truth and those who speak only from the limitation of their own minds.

Part 3
COMING HOME

CREDO

We can spend all our lives trying to pinpoint what we really believe, for our beliefs are in a constant state of flux, affected by new information, new insight, challenges and disturbances, difficulties and developments. Our beliefs need to be flexible; like a river they must flow on until they reach something greater. If movement is obstructed then waters stagnate; so too our minds. What follows, then, is an expression of belief, although I know my own creed will go on changing each time I come back to it, for there is always something new. I took the opening chapter of John's Gospel as inspiration, enjoying the imagery of life and light, grace and the closeness of the Son to his Father's heart. In sharing this personal statement of faith, I seek not so much to persuade you to my way of thinking, as to inspire you to try the exercise for yourself.

I believe in the supreme power of God's love, and the sanctity of life.

I believe in the wisdom we can gain from watching and being with the trees and stones, the moon and sun, the water and fire. In our earthly lives we share the atoms of the universe for our bodies; we are children of the earth, we need to find harmony with the world around us.

I believe in the God of life and light, of the wild, ancient world that began its great wheeling long before people came. I believe in the vibrant Spirit of God which dances within and around all that is, drawing all together.

I believe in the beauty at the heart of each of us, the light of God deep within, which the Spirit compels us to seek out even in the darkest shadows and the most desperate hearts.

I believe some begin to find that light on this earth and live by it, while others rediscover it only when their souls slip from the shells which carry them. Yet we are all journeying together, and we are all called to respond to the needs of our fellows.

I believe in one who knew the light of God within so well that his wisdom and courage, compassion and depth made him shine like a beacon in the dark. This man they called Jesus, Yeshua.

He is our brother, our teacher, our inspiration. He, above all, walked this path for the good of others, demonstrating once and for all the worth of every last and lost soul. In dying, Jesus's broken body set free the Spirit of God for all, that we too might learn to sense God's presence with us. Jesus, from his home in the heart of God, speaks still and loves still. Even now we can ask our brother to walk with us, talk with us, guide and forgive us. Even now we are dependent on the grace which he came to proclaim.

I believe in the Spirit of God, the dynamic, creative Power of the Greatest Good, the voice of God in Genesis that hovered over the primal waters at the beginning of time, ushering in all that God found good. Here is the energy that sows seeds of hope amidst the despair, order amidst the chaos, peace amidst the violence, and love amidst the fear and anger with which we otherwise live. It is this power that disturbs us and challenges us, compelling us to go out like sheep among wolves, into the most shadowy corners of this earth, to be vehicles of God's healing love. It is this power that gives us the will to follow Christ through the narrow door.

The Spirit of God has myriad aspects, many names: Spirit of Grace, Spirit of Truth, Spirit of Peace, Spirit of Wisdom. The Spirit of God, by whatever name, lives with us and in us, and is the energy with which we and all creation vibrate. It is the will behind our journey home, back to the infinite heart of God.

I believe the Spirit is of God and is God. She is always to be recognised, for she speaks with a voice of compassion, gentleness, strength and forgiveness of our human weakness. It is this forgiveness that we need in order to be made whole.

Thus, God, the Power of Love, shines on like the sun, and enfolds us back into the heart as we in our turn recall our home and wish to return. Like the prodigal son we are welcomed and forgiven. The Spirit of God is never separate from God but is that which reaches out to us like sunbeams to touch our lives with warmth and peace, and to live in our own hearts so that we are never alone. Christ, the spiritual presence of Jesus, the human translator of God's love, offers a bridge, a guiding hand, a light in the dark.

Some say Christ will return to earth one day. I believe Christ is returning and has been returning in every act of selfless love and compassion, every word spoken for the sake of healing since Jesus's death. Any who live knowing God is at their heart follow in the footsteps of Jesus and carry the light of Christ as a comfort and strength for others, whatever name they choose to give their power.

I believe in searching out a spiritual path, to enrich life and motivate selflessness, to dive deeper into life. We are surrounded by a wealth of wisdom and love: we have been given a message of forgiveness and inclusion: we have God within and Christ beside us as we seek out our sealskin and return home.

CONCLUSION

'Let the heavens be glad, and let the earth rejoice;
let the sea roar and all that fills it;
let the field exult, and everything in it.
Then shall the trees of the forest sing for joy
before the Lord; for he is coming,
for he is coming to judge the world with righteousness,
and the peoples with his truth.'

— Psalm 96:11–13 (NRSV)

Why should the earth be so glad that the Lord is coming to judge, when the thought of judgement day strikes fear into the hearts of men and women alike? The quotation above from Psalm 96 makes the event sound more like prize day. Yet creation (minus most of humanity) is overjoyed at the prospect of truth being declared, for it has nothing to hide. The natural world has never spoken anything but the truth and can only be in harmony with the greater voice of God. It is a celebration of life; there is no cause for the natural world to be afraid. This is why we can look with confidence to the living world around us for insight into the deeper meaning of our own lives.

We fear judgement because we know that we have the gift of autonomy, we have the power to think, make decisions and choose how we live. We have morality, and therefore we have little excuse for immorality. For those who believe that the earth came into existence in order that humans might develop, it is a bitter pill to swallow to admit that the darlings of creation behave like spoilt children and wreak havoc without stopping to consider the consequences. We might well fear judgement day, knowing that the human race, on the whole, has behaved very like the prodigal son. We have taken the wealth for ourselves and squandered it; we are now starting to look to a future when resources will eventually dwindle. Our hedonism has gone too far and of course we baulk at the prospect of being told that we must stop our excesses.

Are we really still experimenting, testing out the rules to see how much we can get away with? We can read the books of the Prophets and find the same story, thousands of years ago. Or are we as a whole moving into a more responsible attitude where we are more ready to listen to others and restrain our impulsiveness? Certainly there are pockets of wisdom-filled thinking in communities and centres around the globe, and in the hearts of many an individual, whether lonely or surrounded by like-minded souls. We must work towards the spread of this light, this wise thought, so that the minds of all people might be inspired and changed by warm rays of truth, interlinked like a sparking cobweb, a Galilean fishing net of hope. It is for those who sense themselves to be part of the network to work towards spreading the light. We are charged with the task of feeding the flame, of letting the Christ-light grow, of taking our lamp from under its cover and letting the flame dance on every wall and in every dark corner. It is those sinister corners that most need our ministry: the places that go unnoticed; the places where timid people shy away in fear; the corners where the rejects of society still curl away, now as they did in the time of Jesus. It takes courage to bear the light. But if we believe in the presence of Christ and, more than that, sense the presence, then we find the strength to go where others fear to walk, to speak when others keep silence, to love those on whom most would turn their backs. The strength we find in Christ must be used in outreach or it is wasted: a lamp under a basket. In walking in the light of Christ we become a city built on a hill. We cannot hide, or we deny what we have become. As the net spreads wider and wider, perhaps we will witness the spiritual maturation of our society; maybe we can usher in a new attitude of mutual respect and Christ-like care. Maybe we will see a change within our lifetimes. Maybe!

There have been changes though; there have been huge triumphs of good over self-centred ignorance. We can look back and see the end of slavery, the reform of prisons, the right for women to vote, the creation of the United Nations and democracy, the end of apartheid; the humble acceptance that in the past our culture behaved cruelly and greedily in its conquest of vulnerable peoples, as it lusted for the glory of empire-building. At least it is recognised now that what we used to call 'primitive', and despise for lack of material advancement, often had much from which we could learn, as in the case of Native American culture(s). But the Native Americans learned their wisdom the hard way: there were peoples amongst them who wiped out whole species and died out themselves through warfare and mismanagement of the environment. The tribes that survived were the remnant, the ones who developed an ethos that stood the test of time. We should not over-idealise the teachings of the Native American people, or the Celts, or any other people, for often there was cruelty and violence in their lifestyles too. But we should listen and learn, and we should pray that we might look to the past and to the diversity of cultures for insight. We should pray that our lives will change, together, for the common good.

Going back to the prodigal son, we can sense how ashamed he must have felt. Not only was he destitute, he had also wiped the family name in the mud of a pig farm and spent his father's hard-earned wealth on loose living. He knew what he had done, and at least he was sorry. Here are we, doing the same with the gifts God has blessed us with, and all too often we don't even realise there is anything to be sorry about. This ignorance is a residue of the old belief that the world must surely be here simply for our benefit – we can treat it as our plaything for it is humans that are important. This attitude is reflected verbatim in the *Natural History* of Pliny the Elder, writing nearly two thousand years ago, who stated that bees were the most marvellous of creatures for they were created solely to provide us with honey. Now, in the moments when we actually stop and think, we do at least acknowledge the great interdependence of life, of which we are but a part. Maybe we have started to learn a little humility. Maybe we are starting to grow up after all. But where do we go next? The prodigal son took himself off home to throw himself on the mercy of his father, feeling it was better to be but a servant in his father's house than to continue as he was. Where can we go? We can't go anywhere; we can't take ourselves to God, for where is God's dwelling? That's why we say we are waiting for God to come here. But God is here already. There is only a journey in our own minds; we need to make a great U-turn and stop the old habits, stop the old selfishness, stop the old negativity and cynicism. And notice that the analogy Jesus made was of going home. The young man went back to the place where he belonged. That's what we can hope for too. On arrival, the lad expected to be punished; he knew he deserved it. Yet he had underestimated his father's endless love and forgiveness. The father understood immediately what had happened. He probably already knew, for gossip travels fast. Despite having been made a laughing stock by his son, he said not a word in criticism, but hurried forward to welcome him with robes and rings. Do we dare hope for such a welcome? Jesus said over and over again that this is what we can expect when we decide to come back.

God loves us like a father loves a missing son, and God waits longingly for us to decide to come back. Sometimes we do need spiritual rescue; we have to call out from where we are, because we have lost the power to help ourselves. But often we can make some attempt to go half way ourselves. That intention is what God waits to see. It is the language of our hearts that God hears. God waits for us to be sorry, waits for us to start the long and lonely walk of humility, and then comes rushing out to greet us. This is as true for people who have already been judged by society to have sinned, such as the corrupt tax collectors of the New Testament, prostitutes and adulterers, as it is true for those seen to be pillars of the community. We only have to see that we were wrong, be sorry, and set our feet towards home, for God suddenly to be there with us, pushing good things into our hands. That is the point where we too can join with creation in rejoicing. Perhaps there is only rejoicing when the Lord comes, because the Lord, like the kind father, waits for us to remember him and want to be with him. The difficulty is in allowing ourselves to believe we are acceptable to God, particularly when we feel we have been *really* bad. There is a need to feel we have atoned or been punished. When we look at people who we know have wronged us, we often want them to be punished too. Well, guilt can punish like living hell in the heart of someone who regrets their error; we are capable of making ourselves feel very sorry indeed. I suspect that this remorse is a necessary experience that comes to us if not in this life then in the next, before we can ever experience the exultation of feeling freed from sin. Sin itself, the very act of error, of going astray, becomes a means by which we can come to discover, like the woman in Luke's Gospel who wept at Jesus's feet, an amplified feeling of gratitude and grace. But the side-effect of guilt is that it places us in separation from God. It is like a great, bolted door. We cut ourselves off, because we know we are so unworthy. Guilt, having been experienced, needs to be removed. We cannot live the lie of separation from God for ever. God is like the sun. Nothing but the imperishable can come near, for the sun's radiance incinerates everything else like chaff. Our impurities will indeed be burned away, and maybe it will hurt. Many a woman knows she is going to feel pain if she becomes pregnant and gives birth, yet still she will long for a child. The outcome is so intrinsically rewarding, so precious, that it seems worth enduring the sensation of being ripped apart. Fear of the pain does not stop the incredible regenerative forces of life; the pain is faced and endured. A woman grasps with every fibre of her being what it is to be human and to have courage, to know the depth of life and love. The pain of labour is like the pain of soul-cleansing, the pain of newness breaking through in the face of the resistance of the self-centred ego. The closer our wrongs are to our self-image, the more of a wrench we will feel. But our iniquities are not the part of us that is of Spirit; we do not need them. The fire of truth leaves that which is of lasting value; the kernel at our heart is safe.

In the story of the flood, the ancient Israelite deity Yahweh judged the earth in a terrible way, causing a holocaust. Yet after the flood, so the myth tells us, a rainbow appeared. The rainbow reminds us of the ancient confidence that outright destruction would not happen again. It was a sign of hope, of promise. We can see in that rainbow the assurance of God's grace, the belief that God will not destroy us despite our failures, but will cleanse and restore. Thus, we can take our rightful place in creation as stewards, and we can share in creation's exuberance, for God comes to earth whenever a heart turns to God. Let us fear no more, but work together to bring, if I dare call it such, a 'new age'. While I hesitate to use such a loaded term, it continues to have meaning, despite recent associations. Yet the newness that we need must not mean turning our backs on society and refusing to take up responsible positions where real changes can be made. It must not include living off the hard work of others without making a genuine contribution in return; nor empty beliefs and superficial quasi-mysticism, but real depth, care and an adult sense of responsibility. Let us prepare our children to be wise where we were foolish, to work for good where we were indifferent, to see clearly with those three eyes, where we were blind. Let us trust that we are loved and are free to love the world, for the world salutes God with joy.

The truth that God comes to declare is the truth of the moment, for all that is past melts away, and all that is in the future is but speculation. God speaks of the present moment, and for souls who have set their feet towards home, the judgement is joyful; for every soul who has turned back to God can speak only of love, gratitude and peace. I see the coming of the Lord into a person's heart as the eternal reliving of the moment when the joyful father sees that his son wants to return and rushes out, thinking only of welcome and restoration. God's voice of truth says, 'This is my child who was lost, but now is found! Rejoice!' People who live close to the 'kingdom' live in the knowledge that the Father loves them.

The decision to change, to come back to God, is the act of putting on the sealskin and diving into the water. The decision requires courage, for the possibility of failure or rejection seems real. But the father of the prodigal son did not reject him, he brought out his best robe as a sign of restored sonship; that robe is the sealskin. The robe, the sealskin, is held out to us. We are invited, even compelled, to put it on, to resume our place in the family home, as beloved children of the Father.

At the start of this book, in the introduction, I asked a question: Who took away the sealskin? I repeat the question, but this time in the context of the Prodigal Son. Who took his robe away in the first place? Having spent his wealth, *he* sold the robe, and in so doing he sold his soul. He gave away his sealskin and thus met true poverty, to the point where he was no longer his own master. He was forced into servitude, even 'godless' servitude, for no person of his own religion would keep pigs. He had nobody to blame but himself and neither do we, except that his awareness of his father was still strong, but our awareness of God is clouded and unreliable. We can of course go on indefinitely accepting filth as our fate, allowing ourselves to become demoralised and visionless, but the ocean calls out, offering to cleanse and comfort. It wants us to dive into its depth and be filled with peace. We have a choice. We can pretend that we don't belong. We can go on denying the selkie in us. But as long as we do that, there will be a longing, an unaccountable yearning; we will never truly be at peace. But always the ocean is there, and when at last we come – for we all will come back in the end – it roars in delight; the huge roar of a cheering crowd. For in reclaiming our sealskin we have declared our soul's desire to belong in God, and at that moment in time God's judgement is not fearsome but joyful. The past is gone already; the pain is gone. The only truth is that we are back where we belong, because we chose to be there. That is the final triumph of free will; that is true reason to rejoice.

SOME USEFUL BOOKS

Celtic Daily Prayer from the Northumbrian Community. HarperCollins, 2000.

Listening for the Heartbeat of God: A Celtic Spirituality, J. Philip Newell. SPCK, 1997.

The Religion of Jesus the Jew, Geza Vermes. SCM Press, 1993.
(Also *Jesus the Jew* and *Jesus and the World of Judaism*.)

Celtic Christianity and Nature, Mary Low. Edinburgh University Press, 1996.

Celts and Christians, Mark Atherton (ed). University of Wales Press, 2002.

Journeys at the Edge: The Celtic Tradition, Tom O'Loughlin. Darton, Longman & Todd, 2000.

Celtic Christianity: Making Myths, Chasing Dreams, Ian Bradley. Edinburgh University Press, 1999.

ABOUT THE AUTHOR

Annie Heppenstall-West was born in Yorkshire in 1969 and brought up in the Midlands. She studied theology at Cambridge University, and then worked as a teacher for ten years in an inner-city area of northern England, specialising in Religious Education, Art and Music. The contemplations in this her first book have arisen out her own quest for spiritual meaning, and she is, she says, still trying to focus on 'the old challenge of how to live an ordinary life in a spiritual way'.

THE IONA COMMUNITY

The Iona Community, founded in 1938 by the Revd George MacLeod, then a parish minister in Glasgow, is an ecumenical Christian community committed to seeking new ways of living the Gospel in today's world. Initially working to restore part of the medieval abbey on Iona, the Community today remains committed to 'rebuilding the common life' through working for social and political change, striving for the renewal of the church with an ecumenical emphasis, and exploring new, more inclusive approaches to worship, all based on an integrated understanding of spirituality.

The Community now has over 240 Members, about 1500 Associate Members and around 1500 Friends. The Members – women and men from many denominations and backgrounds (lay and ordained), living throughout Britain with a few overseas – are committed to a fivefold Rule of devotional discipline, sharing and accounting for use of time and money, regular meeting, and action for justice and peace.

At the Community's three residential centres – the Abbey and the MacLeod Centre on Iona, and Camas Adventure Camp on the Ross of Mull – guests are welcomed from March to October and over Christmas. Hospitality is provided for over 110 people, along with a unique opportunity, usually through week-long programmes, to extend horizons and forge relationships through sharing an experience of the common life in worship, work, discussion and relaxation. The Community's shop on Iona, just outside the Abbey grounds, carries an attractive range of books and craft goods.

The Community's administrative headquarters are in Glasgow, which also serves as a base for its work with young people, the Wild Goose Resource Group working in the field of worship, a bi-monthly magazine, *Coracle*, and a publishing house, Wild Goose Publications.

For information on the Iona Community contact:
The Iona Community
Fourth Floor, Savoy House, 140 Sauchiehall Street,
Glasgow G2 3DH, UK
Phone: +44 (0)141 332 6343
e-mail: ionacomm@gla.iona.org.uk   web: www.iona.org.uk

For enquiries about visiting Iona, please contact:
Iona Abbey
Isle of Iona
Argyll PA76 6SN, UK
Phone: +44 (0)1681 700404   e-mail: ionacomm@iona.org.uk

ALPHABETICAL INDEX OF CONTEMPLATIONS

Air

Alder tree

Altar

Angel

Apple tree

Arrow

Ash tree

Axe

Balances

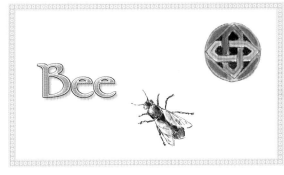

Bee

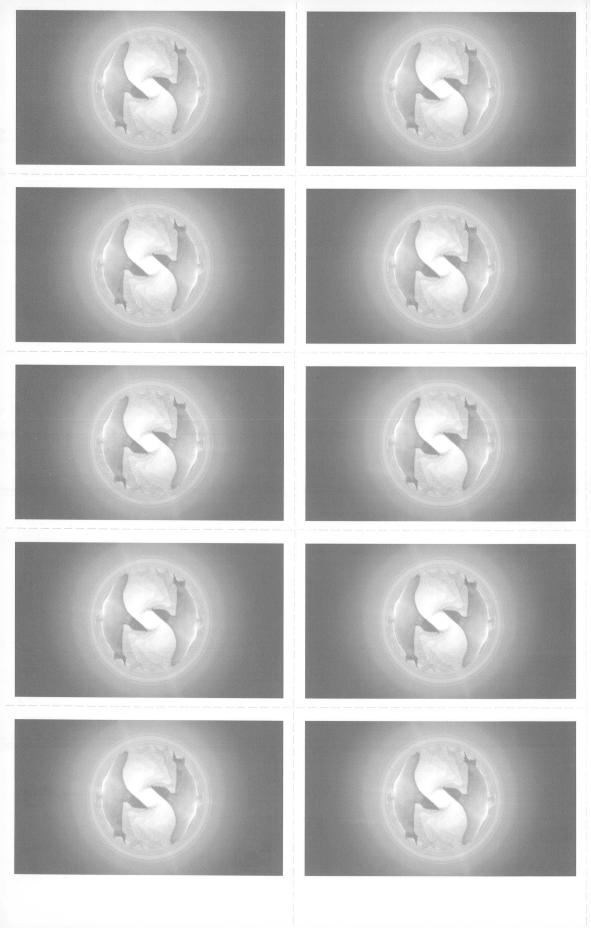

Beech tree

Birch tree

Boat

Bread

Bubble

Butterfly

Cat

Clay

Daisy

Deer

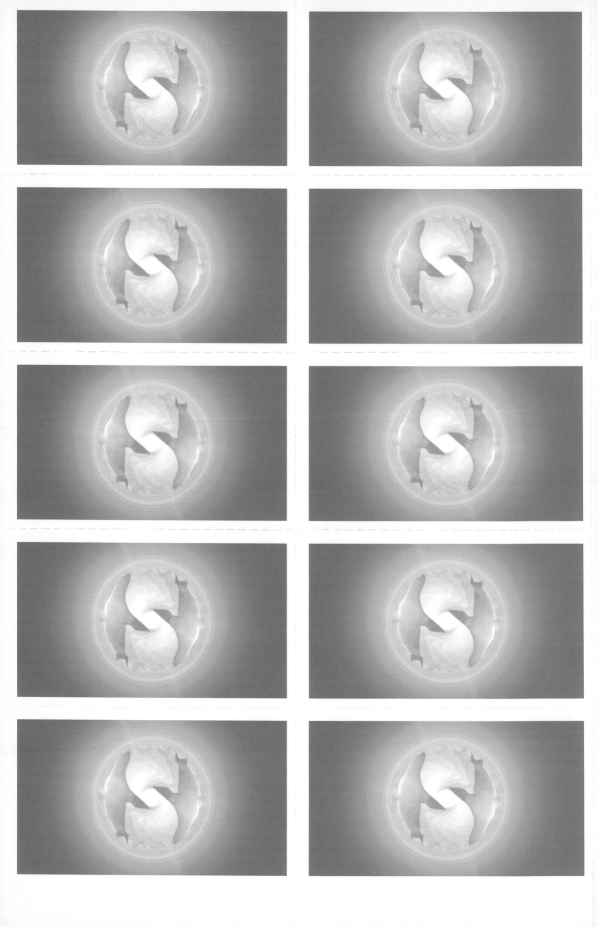

Demon

Dog

Donkey

Door

Feathers

Fire

Fish

Flood

Fox

Hawthorn Tree

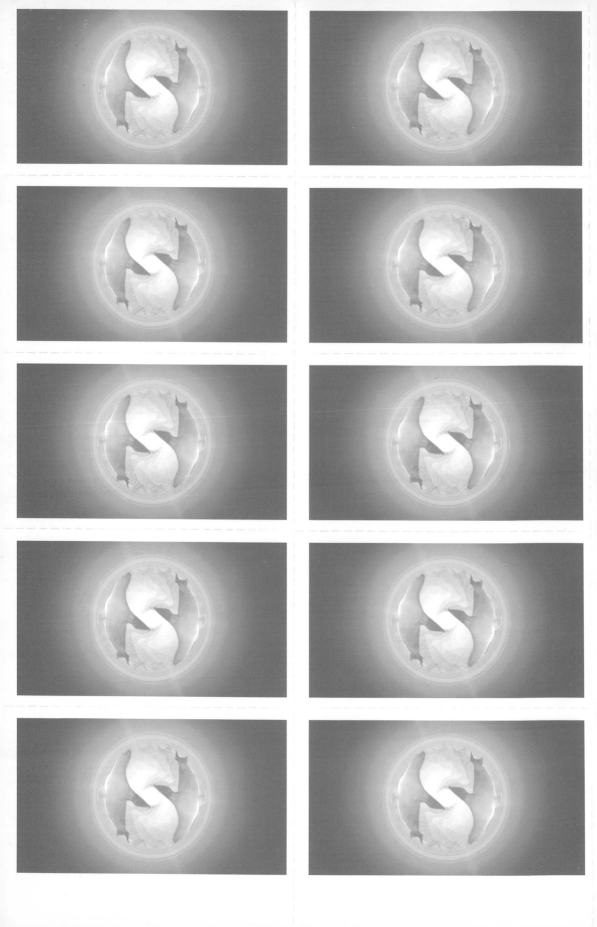

heartbeat

Hen

Holly

Hornbeam tree

Ice

Idol

Lavender

Magpie

Mole

Moon

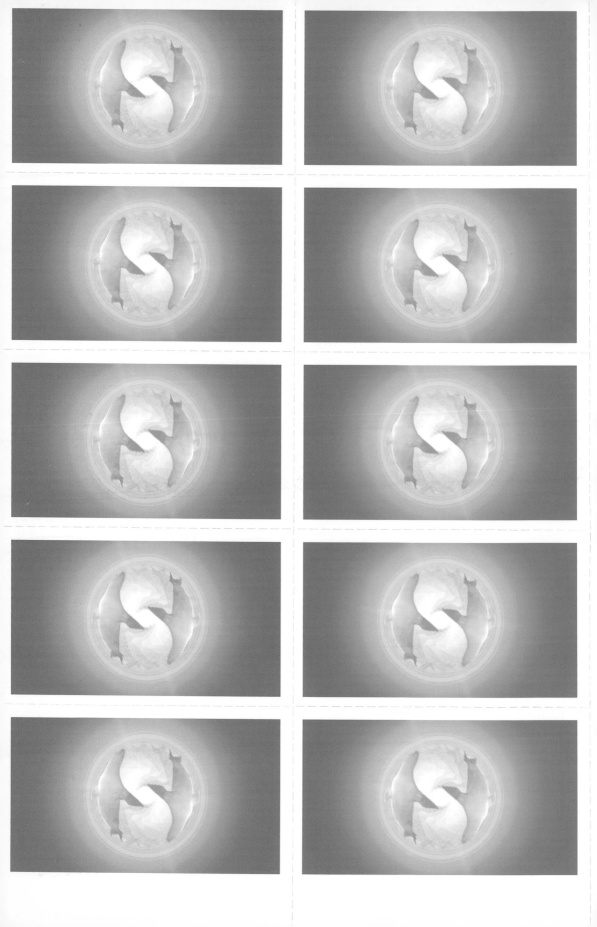

Mountain

Oak tree

Otter

Owl

Pathway

Pig

Pine tree

Pony

Rabbit

Rainbow

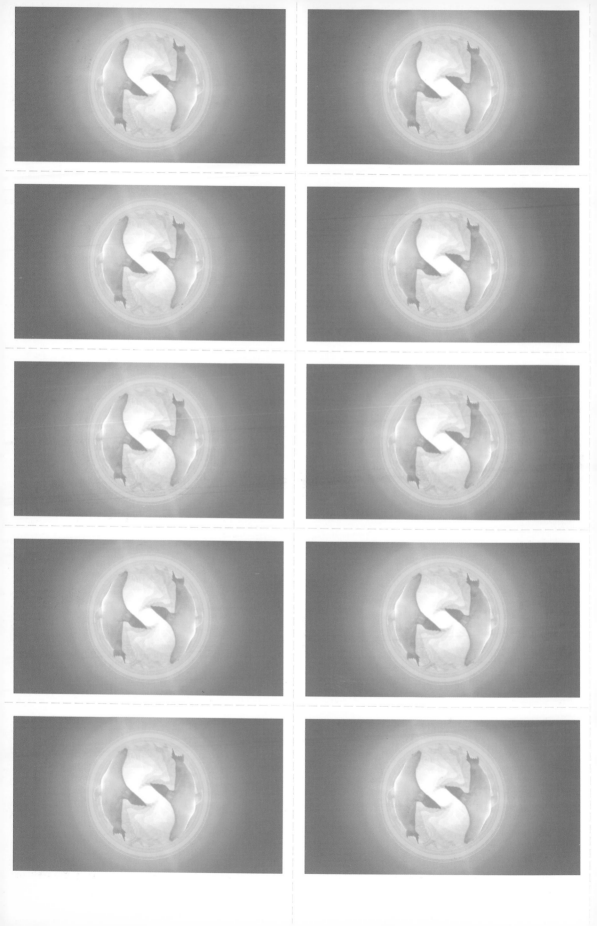

Ripples

Rowan tree

Seal

Seed

Sheep

Shell

Snake

Sparrow & swallow

Spring

Squirrel

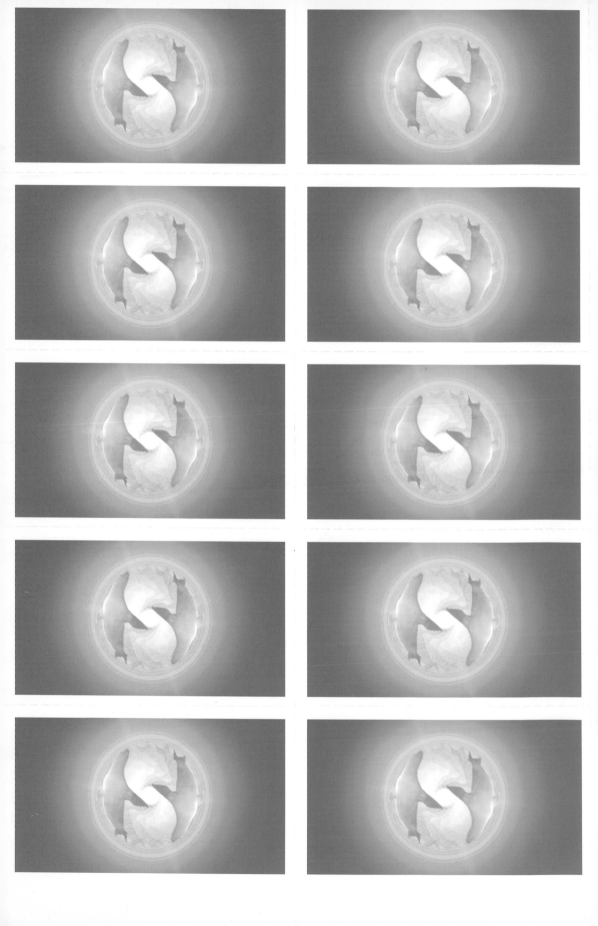

Stone

Sun

Sycamore tree

Tent

Voice

Water

Wilderness

Willow tree

Wolf

Yew tree

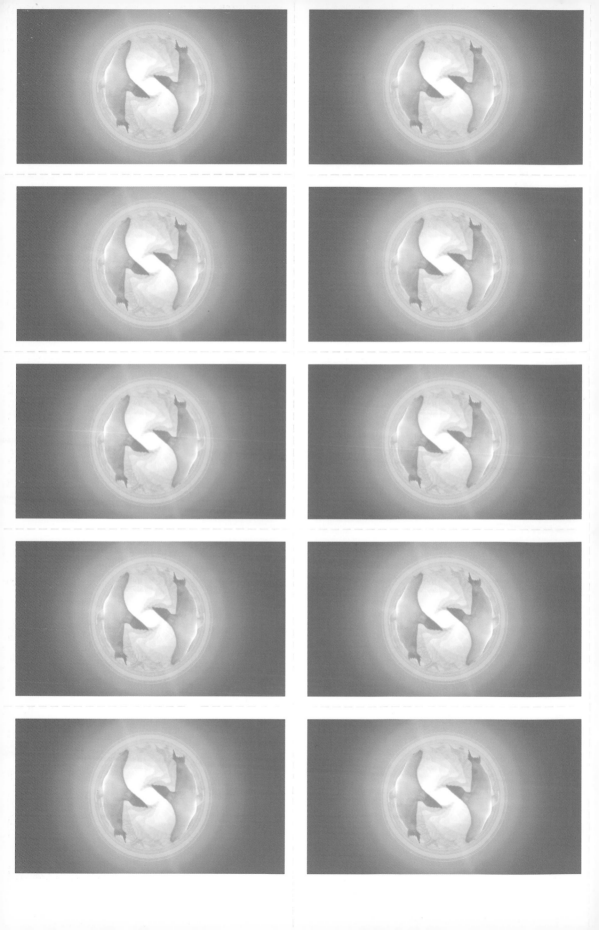